SURVEYS AND EXPERIMENTS IN EDUCATION RESEARCH

SURVEYS AND EXPERIMENTS IN EDUCATION RESEARCH

James F. McNamara, Ph.D.

Texas A&M University

TECHNOMIC
PUBLISHING CO., INC.

LANCASTER · BASEL

Surveys and Experiments in Education Research

a **TECHNOMIC**®publication

Published in the Western Hemisphere by
Technomic Publishing Company, Inc.
851 New Holland Avenue, Box 3535
Lancaster, Pennsylvania 17604 U.S.A.

Distributed in the Rest of the World by
Technomic Publishing AG
Missionsstrasse 44
CH-4055 Basel, Switzerland

Printed in the United States of America
10 9 8 7 6 5 4 3

Main entry under title:
  Surveys and Experiments in Education Research

A Technomic Publishing Company book
Bibliography: p.

Library of Congress Catalog Card No. 94-60492
ISBN No. 1-56676-167-0

*To Maryanne, Paul, Raymond,
Julianne and Neil*

TABLE OF CONTENTS

SCHOOL administrators in America are under tremendous pressures to improve schools and pupil learning. New reform legislation requires them to expand the umbrella of involvement with parents and teachers in planning and budget development. It also requires that administrators understand how to find out what their various stakeholder groups really want to see happen in their schools. Thus, the importance of the survey as well-constructed, accurate, valid, and reliable is more crucial than ever before in the successful operation of schools.

Planning school reform means administrators will have to understand experimental research approaches, know how to define the most important problems, recognize the important design issues, and know how to interpret the data they gain from the surveys and research they undertake.

Jim McNamara is the kind of teacher that is the practitioner's dream. He sees not only with the eyes of the researcher, but he understands the problems of the practitioner. He is not only grounded in all of the mathematical and statistical knowledge necessary, but he writes with broad strokes of common sense and insight to the ongoing problems administrators confront in doing research and surveys in real schools. He has other qualities that should endear him to his readers: he writes clearly, and his work is thoroughly linked to the best thinking and practice in the field. Even a casual perusal of his work will reveal how meticulously Jim McNamara pursues a point and provides examples that are understandable.

It's rare to find all of these remarkable qualities in a writer of statistical and research works today. Jim McNamara knows how to retain content integrity while making his subject "user friendly." Try reading McNamara's sections on sample sizes, statistical power, and the effect size criterion in school improvement research, and you will be struck as to the imminent practicality of his approach. These are questions asked by nearly all doctoral-level students and serious practitioners working in reform-legislated states. My prediction is that not only will Jim McNamara's work have an impact on school-based surveys and research, it will also change the way college- and university-based courses are taught, as well as when these topics are discussed.

The most remarkable thing about Jim McNamara's work is that he has removed the fear that robs so much from research, and this results in an impact in changing real schools. By making what can be arcane understandable, practical, and sensible, there is hope that not only will research begin to inform practice, but that practice will finally change its habits. At that point, we may have realized that there is and never was a "theory-practice" gap. All practice is informed by some theory. We may, at last, attempt to discern and describe why schools and the administrators and teachers in them do what they do.

FENWICK W. ENGLISH
Professor, College of Education
University of Kentucky
Lexington, Kentucky

WHEN I accepted the summer 1991 offer to become the research editor of the *International Journal of Educational Reform (IJER)*, the journal editor asked me to develop a quarterly column that would help readers link research with educational reform efforts. While far more could have been said about how to create this linkage, no more specific expectations or detailed instructions were advanced. Thus, I was challenged to create my own linkage strategy.

This book is the result. It brings together, in a single source, my first seven quarterly columns. Each of these seven columns deals with one of the two research methods most likely to be used in school improvement research projects: *surveys and experiments*.

WHY THIS BOOK EMPHASIZES SCHOOL IMPROVEMENT AND RESEARCH METHODS

Two key questions were used to guide the directions taken in creating these seven columns. Both questions deserve mention here since they reveal important insights about the role of research in educational reform efforts. In addition, the responses to these two questions offer insights into the scope and sequence of these seven columns.

Put briefly, the first question was as follows: If you were asked to use a single sentence to describe the purpose of educational reforms, what would you say? For me, the answer was straight-forward. Educational reforms are efforts to improve schools and schooling. With this response in hand, I decided that my initial *IJER* columns would focus specifically on school improvement research. This focus still remains as I am now working on the four quarterly research columns for the third volume of *IJER*.

The second question I formulated dealt with the distinction between consumers of research and producers of research. Specifically, I posed this question: Should my initial efforts to link research and educational reform projects concentrate on (A) illustrating how research methods can be used effectively to discover and evaluate new interventions or (B) describing how one goes about adopting interventions that prior research has already shown to be effective in other schools having similar characteristics and problems?

Strictly speaking, these two options are not independent. However, there is a critical difference. *Option A* centers on thinking in terms of producers of research. It involves using behavioral science research methods to uncover new interventions or policy preferences. *Option B*, on the other hand, centers on consumers of research. It shifts interest from inventing new improvement strategies to selecting established interventions.

While both options are important and provide unique perspectives for linking research with reform efforts, I chose *Option A* (as indicated in the title) for two primary reasons.

First, I believe that advancing knowledge in any profession is greatly enhanced when we are able to view both theorists and practitioners as producers of research. My position has always been favorable to this notion. Suggesting that all research contributions to a profession's knowledge base should be produced by either university professors or policy analysts residing in research and development centers tends to overlook the unique insights and contributions of practitioner scholars.

Second, a review of existing educational research methods texts reveals a real need to provide meaningful examples of how research methods can be used in actual practicing professional environments. Most examples found in current educational research methods texts illustrate either how theorists conduct empirical validation studies or how graduate students conduct traditional dissertation research. While such examples usually illustrate correct ways to use research tools and techniques, they almost always fail to capture how research methods can be adapted or modified to account for realistic constraints encountered in decision-oriented inquiries commissioned by policymakers and practitioners.

HOW THIS BOOK CAN BE USED

This book is aimed at a rather broad audience—anyone interested in conducting and/or evaluating behavioral science surveys and experiments. More specifically, it is aimed at five distinct audiences: (1) methodology students, (2) beginning researchers, (3) university professors and policy analysts who wish to become more actively involved with practitioners in collaborative research ventures, (4) education and human services professionals who are responsible for commissioning and later evaluating decision-oriented research projects, and (5) teacher researchers who see conducting school improvement research projects as a valuable way to increase their effectiveness in the classroom.

These are the same five audiences I kept in mind when writing my first seven *IJER* research columns. For this reason, I have elected to reproduce each column exactly as it appeared in the journal. Accordingly, the book has seven chapters.

The sequence of the chapters in the book corresponds to the sequence of research columns in *IJER*. Thus, Chapter 1 was originally published in Volume 1, Number 1. Chapter 2 was published in Volume 1, Number 2, and so forth. To maintain the correspondence between the book and *IJER*, the chapter titles are identical to those used in the journal.

A quick glance at any chapter will uncover a common pattern. Each chapter has a text whose organization is elaborated in the beginning of the chapter. Each chapter also has a notes section, which is printed in full size type. The purpose of the note section is to extend the information on basic ideas introduced in the chapter and to provide a few guidelines for those who wish to do more advanced reading on a topic of interest.

Taken collectively, the seven notes sections provide a detailed roadmap for anyone seeking to engage in independent study on using surveys and experiments in schools and other human service organizations.

It is important for readers to recognize that the chapters can be read in any order. In this regard, both the overlaps in the coverage and the directions in the notes referring readers to specific sections in earlier *IJER* columns should prove to be very helpful.

Six suggestions are offered below to help readers design their individual plans for creating the order in which they might read the seven chapters.

Research Design

Methodology students whose primary interests are sampling designs and the corresponding required sample sizes should read the first four chapters in their original order. Put briefly, the first three chapters address specific sampling design concerns. Chapter 4 reviews these concerns and, thus, serves as a summary for the research design and sampling guidelines given in the three earlier chapters.

Survey Research

Beginning researchers interested primarily in an overview of basic issues and concerns in survey research should first concentrate on reading Chapters 5 through 7. These three chapters can be read in any order, but I would recommend reading them in their natural order, beginning with Chapter 5. Once this has been accomplished, it would be very helpful to next read Chapter 1, which provides explicit guidelines for conducting preference surveys in a single school district.

Experiments

Practitioners and theorists whose first interest is to learn more about conducting meaningful experiments in the schools should first read Chapters 2 and 3. These two chapters make extensive use of a realistic case study that details how to compare traditional (existing) and new (alternate) methods designed to increase student achievement.

Collaborative Research

University professors and policy analysts who wish to join practitioners to conduct decision-oriented research in the schools should first study the policy preference case study (using survey methods) detailed in Chapter 1 and the teaching methods case study (using experimental methods) introduced in Chapter 2. Next, they should read Chapters 3 and 4, which will link these two cases to hypothesis testing and sampling issues frequently encountered in university-based research efforts. The remaining chapters can be read in any order. Special attention should be given to the ethics of reporting research findings, which is covered in the latter part of Chapter 5.

Teacher Researchers

My best advice for teacher researchers would be to begin by following the strategy I outlined above for those whose primary interest is to learn how to conduct meaningful experiments in the schools. Next, I'd recommend following the strategy detailed above for beginning researchers who wish to acquire an overview of basic issues and concerns in survey research.

Other Alternatives

Each of the five previous suggestions is just that—a suggestion. While there are many other ways to order the seven chapters, I'd like to make just one last suggestion. If you have had some prior exposure to basic research methods and statistics and if you plan to read all seven chapters as a means to get a better handle on school improvement research strategies, I would recommend that you begin with Chapter 1 and continue to read the chapters in the order I have presented them in the table of contents. However, don't be afraid to let a recommendation for further reading presented in one of the chapter notes take you on an informative detour. These detours will lead you to some of the very best research methods and statistics sources I have encountered in teaching research methods for the past twenty-three years.

CHAPTER 1

Sample Sizes for School Preference Surveys

IN the early stages of planning a school restructuring effort, it is not uncommon to conduct a preference survey of one or more key stakeholder groups. For example, members involved in a school district restructuring effort that is considering a year-round schooling program might be interested in knowing the preferences of students, parents or guardians, teachers, and voters in the district for starting a year-round school program. Clearly, all of these stakeholders are likely to experience significant changes if a year-round school policy is approved by the district's board of trustees.

The intent of this chapter is to examine how one might go about determining the correct sample size for a policy preference survey that uses probability sampling. Using a straightforward case study, this article will answer three specific sample size questions: (1) Is there a simple table of recommended sample sizes one might use to determine the actual sample size for a policy preference survey? (2) Are there valid ways to reduce the actual sample sizes recommended in these tables? (3) What special problems might need to be considered in reaching a final decision on the actual sample size for the survey? Accordingly, the chapter is divided into three parts, each of which concentrates on one of the questions.

Taken collectively and in the order specified above, answers to these three sampling design questions reveal a straightforward three-step process that will provide a correct sample size solution for a school preference survey.

STEP 1: THE INITIAL SOLUTION

The initial solution, a response to question one, can be illustrated by focusing on a single stakeholder group and just one preference question. Thinking in terms of the school restructuring effort referenced above, let us assume that the members of the planning group wish to estimate the percent of the district's classroom teachers who would prefer to explore the year-round school alternative.

In this case, the questionnaire item for the preference survey might be the following: *This school district is considering a year-round school program. Would you prefer this alternative to our existing nine-month school year? (Yes or No).*

Sampling Design

An appropriate survey sampling design for this case would be a simple random sampling design. To implement this basic probability sampling design, one would begin by constructing a list of all classroom teachers in the district. Numbering the entries in this teacher list would reveal the size of the population (N).

Once N is known, a published sampling table (for example see Krejcie and Morgan, 1970) can be consulted to indicate the recommended sample size (n). Finally, a table of random numbers or a computerized random number generator can be used to select n random numbers between one and N. Teachers whose numbers were selected would then be asked to respond to the preference survey question specified above.

Sampling Tables

An abbreviated (but typical) simple random sampling table is given in Table 1.1. If a school district has 200 classroom teachers, the recommended sample size in Table 1.1 is 132. Thus, N is 200 and n is 132 which represents 66 percent of the classroom teacher population.

Table 1.1. Typical table for determining sample size.

Population (N)	Sample (n)	Sample Percent of Population 100 (n/N)
50	44	88.00
100	80	80.00
200	132	66.00
500	217	43.40
1,000	278	27.80
5,000	357	7.14
10,000	370	3.70
20,000	377	1.89
75,000	382	0.51
1,000,000	384	0.04
2,000,000	384	0.02
Over 2 Million	384	<0.02

Note: This table is an abbreviated version of a typical published sample size table. Table is constructed to yield a 95 percent confidence interval for a margin of error not to exceed 5 percent. It assumes no reliable prior information is known about the true proportion of yes responses in the population of interest.

If a school district of interest is a large urban school district, then N might be 10,000. For this school district, the recommended sample size in Table 1.1 is n equal to 370. In this case the sample size is just 3.7 percent of the population.

A careful examination of Table 1.1 clearly indicates the efficiency of using probability samples. Specifically, the larger the population, the smaller the percent of the population needed in the sample. Moreover, the *maximum* sample size for any population—no matter how large it is—is just 384.

If resources are available to meet the sample size recommended in Table 1.1 and no special considerations arise, the second and third questions (steps two and three) can be skipped, and the sample size problem is sovled.

Programmed Decision

The use of a typical published sample size table to determine the initial (or maybe the final) recommended sample size involves agreement with three preprogrammed survey design decisions. The three preprogrammed decisions, the symbols used to represent them, and the actual preset formula values used to get the recommended sample size of 370 are as follows:

1. *The precision (B)* has been preset at 0.05 to guarantee a margin of error no larger than five percent.
2. *The confidence coefficient (A)* has been preset at 3.84 to indicate the use of a 95 percent confidence interval for reporting the margin of error.
3. *The prior information value (P)* has been preset at 0.50 to indicate that there is no reliable presurvey estimate of the true proportion of yes responses in the population of interest, which in this case is all classroom teachers in the district.

Each of these three preprogrammed design decisions was used to construct Table 1.1. Agreement with these three design decisions (a position taken when one wishes to end the search for a recommended sample size at Step 1) guides the analysis and reporting of the actual survey responses provided by the classroom teachers. This consequence is discussed below.

Survey Findings

For every sample size table, there is a second table that is used to indicate the actual margin of error that results from the analysis of the survey responses. Table 1.2 is the corresponding table for our case study where N is 10,000 and n is 370. Consistent with the predetermined values used in Table 1.1, the survey findings are to be reported using a 95 percent confidence interval for the margin of error.

Table 1.2 has a straightforward interpretation. If the actual percent of yes responses for this classroom teacher survey is 55 percent, then we take the position that the correct percent for the population that includes all classroom teachers in the district is between 50 percent and 60 percent (see Note 1).

While only one percentage value will result from conducting a survey, it is important to recognize that the actual sample percent of *yes* responses can be any value between zero and 100.

Table 1.2. Precision values for possible sample proportions.

Sample Proportion (p)	Sample Percent (100 p)	Margin of Error (%)	Confidence Interval	
			Low (%)	High (%)
0.50	50	5.0	45.0	55.0
0.55	55	5.0	50.0	60.0
0.60	60	4.9	55.1	64.9
0.65	65	4.7	60.3	69.7
0.70	70	4.6	65.4	74.6
0.75	75	4.3	70.7	79.3
0.80	80	4.2	75.8	84.2
0.85	85	3.6	81.4	88.6
0.90	90	3.0	87.0	93.0
0.95	95	2.2	92.8	97.2
0.99	99	1.0	98.0	100.0

Note: Table was constructed for a sample of 370 from a population of 10,000. Entries can be interpreted as follows. If the sample percent of yes responses is 55 percent, the margin of error is 5 percent and the 95 percent confidence interval for the true proportion of yes responses in the population is between 45 percent and 55 percent. For sample values less than 50 percent, use the same distance above 50 percent. For example, if the sample percent is 10 percent, use the 90 percent entry. In this case, the margin of error is 3 percent and the confidence interval ranges from a low of 7 percent to a high of 13 percent.

Thus p, the corresponding sample proportion, could range from zero to one.

Table 1.2 is constructed to cover all of these possibilities. For example, if the actual percent of *yes* responses for classroom teachers in the sample is 85 percent, the margin of error would be 3.6 percent and the confidence interval to estimate the true percent of *yes* responses for the classroom teacher population would range from 81.4 percent to 88.6 percent (see Note 2).

A careful examination of Table 1.2 exhibits a very important sampling design consequence. Specifically, the margin of error for implementing the simple random sampling design where N is 10,000 and n is 370 will *never* exceed five percent. However, as the actual percent of *yes* responses in the sample increases, the corresponding margin of error decreases.

Sampling Error

It is important to recognize that a margin of error table is needed for any probability sampling survey one chooses to imple-

Table 1.3. Estimating the margin of error using a 95 percent confidence interval.

Step 1:	Evaluate pq = the product of p and q.
Step 2:	Determine $U = pq \div n$.
Step 3:	Calculate $F = (N - n) \div N$.
Step 4:	Evaluate V = the product of U and F.
Step 5:	Determine S = the square root of V.
Step 6:	Evaluate M = the product of 1.96 and S.

p = the actual proportion of *yes* responses in the sample.

$q = (1 - p)$.

U = the unadjusted variance of the estimator p.

F = the finite corrected factor (fcf).

N = the size of the population.

n = the size of the sample.

V = the adjusted variance of the estimator p using (fcf).

S = the standard error of p.

M = the margin of error with 95 confidence coefficient.

Note: If 99 percent confidence interval is desired, replace 1.96 with 2.57. If 90 percent confidence interval is desired, the replacement value in Step 6 is 1.64. All three of these values are the square roots of A which is tabled value of chi-squared for one degree of freedom at the desired significance level. For 95 percent confidence interval, the corresponding significance level is 0.05.

ment. With this requirement in mind, Table 1.3 provides a step-by-step procedure the school district planning committee can use to determine the margin of error values reported in Table 1.2.

Application of this procedure is illustrated in Table 1.4 for the situation where the actual proportion of *yes* responses for the 370 classroom teacher responses is 55 percent. Notice that this Table 1.4 illustration yields a margin of error of five percent, which is

Table 1.4. Calculating a margin of error.

Step 1:	$pq = (0.55)(0.45) = 0.2475$
Step 2:	$U = 0.2475/370 = 0.000669$
Step 3:	$F = (10{,}000 - 370)/10{,}000 = 0.96300$
Step 4:	$V = (U)(F) = 0.000644$
Step 5:	S = Square Root of $V = 0.0254$
Step 6:	$M = (1.96)(0.0254) = 0.05$ (or 5 percent)

Note: Since proportions rather than integers are used, accuracy to at least six decimal places is required in steps 2 through 4. Values in the last step are usually rounded to two or three decimal places. This table is to be read in conjunction with Table 1.3.

the actual Table 1.2 value reported on line two for p equal to 0.55.

Reflections on Step 1

The use of a published sample size table in Step 1 provides a quick and valid solution to the sample size problem. However, if standard guidelines for reporting survey research findings are to be followed, there is still the need to report a margin of error for the school preference survey (see Note 3).

Thus, one who wishes to solve the sample size problem using a published table must not only understand the predetermined survey sampling design decisions, but also must be able to use this design information to construct a corresponding estimation table for correctly interpreting and reporting the school preference survey findings (see Note 4).

STEP 2: ALTERNATIVE SOLUTIONS

Assume this urban school district wishes to explore ways to reduce the actual classroom teacher sample size of 370 recommended in Step 1. This exploration involves altering the three preprogrammed decisions used in constructing Table 1.1.

To understand the consequences of altering the preprogrammed decisions used in Step 1, it is essential to know how the three decision values are related. These relationships are determined by the basic sample size formula elaborated in Table 1.5.

The basic sample size formula elaborated in Table 1.5 is used to construct any published sample size table for a simple random sample focusing on the percent of *yes* responses in a population of interest.

This sample size formula was used to construct Table 1.1. It can be verified by setting P at 0.50, A at 3.84 and B at 0.05. Substituting these values into the formula along with N equal to 10,000 yields a recommended classroom teacher sample size of 370, which is exactly the value entered in Table 1.1. These

Table 1.5. *The basic sample size formula to estimate a binomial proportion.*

Formula: $n = NPQ \div [(N - 1) D + PQ]$ $D = C \div A$
Legend: N = the population size. n = the recommended sample size. P = the population proportion (which is preset at 0.50 when no prior survey estimate can be given). $Q = (1 - P)$. A = the table value of chi-squared for one degree of freedom at the desired significance level (which is usually preset at 3.84 to yield a significance level of 0.05 and a corresponding confidence coefficient of 0.95 for the confidence interval). B = the desired precision (bound) for the margin of error expressed as a proportion (which is usually preset at 0.05 to yield a confidence interval estimate of plus or minus 5 percent). C = the square of B.

calculations are presented in Table 1.6 using a step-by-step procedure.

Exploration One: Prior Information

When no prior information is available, P is usually set at 0.50. This represents a *maximum* sample size. However, if prior knowledge (i.e., data from previous studies or informed conjectures) is available, n can often be reduced appreciably.

Consider the Table 1.7 formula solutions for this case study. Let A remain constant at 3.84 and B remain constant at 0.05. However, let P be free to vary.

Following the calculation guide given in Table 1.6, the solutions for the first exploration where only P is altered yield an interesting result. Specifically, these solutions clearly indicate that the further one moves away from the predetermined P value of 0.50, the smaller the recommended sample size becomes. For example, if P equals 0.85 rather than 0.50, the recommended

Table 1.6. *Application of the basic sample size formula.*

Initial Calculations:
Step 1: $NPQ = (10,000) (0.50) (0.50) = 2,500$ Step 2: $C = (0.05) (0.05) = 0.0025$ Step 3: $D = C \div A = 0.0025/3.84 = 0.000651$ Step 4: $(N - 1) D = (10,000 - 1) (0.000651) = 6.5097$ Step 5: $PQ = (0.50) (0.50) = 0.25$
Recommended Sample Size (n): $n = NPQ \div [(N - 1) D + PQ]$ $n = 2,500 \div [6.5097 + 0.25] = 370$

Note: Since proportions rather than integers are used, accuracy to six decimal places is needed to get D in Step 3. This exact D value is then used in Step 4.

Table 1.7. *Explorations using the basic sample size formula for N = 10,000.*

Exploration	P	B	A	n
Exploration 1	**0.50**	**0.05**	**3.84**	**370**
(vary only P)	0.60	0.05	3.84	356
	0.70	0.05	3.84	313
	0.75	0.05	3.84	280
	0.80	0.05	3.84	240
	0.85	0.05	3.84	192
Exploration 2	**0.50**	**0.05**	**3.84**	**370**
(vary only B)	0.50	0.06	3.84	260
	0.50	0.07	3.84	192
	0.50	0.08	3.84	148
Exploration 3	0.50	0.05	2.71	264
(vary only A)	**0.50**	**0.05**	**3.84**	**370**
	0.50	0.05	6.63	622

Note: All input values (*P*, *B*, and *A*) and the formula that is used to get the recommended sample size (*n*) are described in Table 1.5 of this article. Table 1.6 illustrates how to use this formula for a population (*N*) equal to 10,000. In each exploration, the typical sample size recommended in published tables is given in bold.

sample size n is 192 rather than 370, which was the only solution in Step 1.

Exploration Two: Precision

Assume the school district restructuring committee might be willing to relax the precision requirements as a means to reduce sample size.

With this alternative in mind, consider the Table 1.7 solutions where P remains constant at 0.50, A remains constant at 3.84 and B is free to vary. This numerical specification represents our willingness to relax the precision requirements.

Solutions for the second exploration indicate that only minor increases in the preprogrammed B value of 0.05 yield large reductions in n. For example, if B equals 0.08 rather than 0.05, the recommended classroom teacher sample size is 148 rather than 370. Thus, altering only this one of the three predetermined values used in Table 1.1 to get our initial solution can result in a sample size reduction of 222 teachers (see Note 5).

Exploration Three: Confidence Coefficient

The Step 1 sample size can also be reduced by changing the confidence coefficient used to report the margin of error.

Consider the Table 1.7 formula solutions where P remains constant at 0.50, B remains constant at 0.05 and A is permitted to vary. This numerical specification represents our willingness to alter the confidence coefficient.

Solutions for this third exploration indicate that reducing only the confidence coefficient will also reduce the recommended sample size. For example, if the alternative confidence coefficient is to be 90 percent (A equals 2.71) rather than 95 percent (A equals 3.84), the sample size of classroom teachers is reduced from 370 teachers to 264 teachers (see Note 6).

Exploration Four: Time Constraints

Assume the district's restructuring committee encounters the following problem. The school trustees plan to make a policy decision regarding year-round schools at their next meeting, which is two days away. Moreover, each trustee has received a small number of phone calls from teacher representatives who either enthusiastically endorse the twelve-month school year or vehemently oppose this alternative. However, no stakeholder group has been surveyed to date. Thus, little is known about the true preferences of the district's classroom teachers.

If one is willing to simultaneously alter all three of the preprogrammed decisions from Step 1, a reduced sample size that allows completion of the survey to meet the two-day deadline could be determined. To do so requires the following numerical specification. First, set P at 0.75. Next, set B at 0.07. Finally, set A at 2.71. This specification will result in a margin of error with a 90 percent confidence interval not likely to exceed seven percent.

Using the basic sample size formula given in Table 1.5, the solution in exploration four is 103. If each of 21 persons were responsible for completing just five brief telephone calls to determine five teacher preferences, this survey could easily meet the two-day time constraints given above (see Note 7).

More important, those who present the survey findings to the school district trustees can speak directly to the validity of their survey results, noting that they used the same scientific sampling procedures required in any of the major national polls such as the Gallup Poll or the *New York Times*/CBS Poll.

Generalizability

The procedure elaborated in Step 2 can be used in any school preference survey where N is given and those responsible for the survey (the school restructuring committee in this case study) are willing to examine in more detail their survey expectations and their three survey sampling decision rules.

STEP 3: SPECIAL CONSIDERATIONS

Two special considerations are often encountered in designing school preference surveys. These two problems and their straightforward solutions are treated in Step 3.

The Multiple Stakeholder Problem

The school district planning committee considering a major policy change, such as the movement from a nine-month to a twelve-month school year, will likely be interested in the preferences held not only by classroom teachers, but also by other school district stakeholders.

If this were the case, a stratified random sample involving all stakeholder groups as individual strata would need to be conducted. To accomplish this objective, one would repeat Steps 1 and 2 for a simple random sampling design for each stratum (see Note 8).

Implementing a stratified random sampling design would allow the restructuring committee to compare the preferences of all stakeholder groups for the year-round school alternative. To ensure adequate statistical power, which is the ability of the survey to detect true preference differences if they do exist among the survey populations of interest, *at least* 100 survey respondents are recommended for each stakeholder group (see Note 9).

The Multiple Item Problem

The school district restructuring committee would probably use more than the one questionnaire item referenced above. To enhance the planning information used to explore year-round schools, the committee might construct additional *yes* or *no* response items. Such items might address individual preferences about year-round program alternatives or beliefs that stakeholders have about how such a program will improve learning, enrich teaching, reduce costs, or provide families a more flexible school schedule (see Note 10).

The sample size solution for the multiple item problem is also straightforward. It follows the procedures elaborated above for Steps 1 and 2. Three specific examples are given below to show how sample size solutions are generated for a questionnaire having two or more yes/no preference items.

Situation One

If no prior information is known about the proportion of the population likely to offer a *yes* response for any of the preference items included in the study, then set P equal to 0.50 for each item. If no changes are required in the predetermined A and B values, the recommended sample sizes in Table 1.1 for Step 1 provide the correct solutions.

Situation Two

If in situation one, there is some interest in reducing the Step 1 solution, then let P remain fixed at 0.50 and examine alternative values for A, B, or both A and B using the basic sample size exploration strategy detailed in Table 1.7.

Situation Three

Assume that no prior preference information is available for some questionnaire items, but prior preference information is available and is deemed to be reliable for other items in the same questionnaire. Strictly speaking, one would need to set P equal to 0.50 so that the margin of error would not exceed the desired level (B) for any item in the questionnaire. This solution was offered in situation one above.

In practical work, however, there is an excellent compromise solution for the multiple item problem. It is to set P equal to 0.75 and proceed to determine what values to use for A and B (see Note 11).

In our case study district (where N equals 10,000), the numerical specification could be P equals 0.75, A equals 3.84 and B equals 0.05. The recommended sample size for the multiple item questionnaire in practical terms is 280. Notice that this is the same sample size we encountered in the first exploration of Step 2 when P was set at 0.75 and the other two predetermined decisions of Table 1.1 were left unchanged.

CONCLUSIONS

Whenever a policy preference survey (or for that matter any needs assessment or program evaluation survey) is to be undertaken as part of a school restructuring effort, serious consideration should be given to using the probability sampling procedures elaborated above rather than using a quota sampling design, a less formal sampling strategy, or a blanket survey that is either forwarded to all members of a stakeholder group or made available to them as a questionnaire published in a local newspaper.

There are several reasons for this position. First, probability samples such as those detailed in this article are almost always no more expensive to implement; in many cases, they are far less expensive to implement than the nonprobability sampling alternatives identified above.

Second, as the three-step procedure demonstrates, the basic sample size formula for probability sampling provides a wide range of recommended sample sizes that can accommodate the specific needs of any planning group.

Third, it is extremely difficult, and in some cases almost impossible, to identify the nonresponse bias that follows from implementing a nonprobability sampling design. In a probability sampling design this bias is defined, and, in many cases, can be accurately estimated.

Finally, and most important, only probability samples can yield true margins of error to guide inferences about a population using data from samples. These margins of error not only are informative but also are required to meet the standard ethical guidelines for reporting survey findings.

NOTES

Note 1 – Throughout the text references to notes are inserted. The text can be read without reference to these notes. Their purpose is threefold: to extend the information provided on basic theoretical concepts, to identify a few noteworthy sources on survey sampling theory, and to specify a few guidelines for readers who may wish to conduct a school preference survey.

In reporting these survey findings, the actual statement for this 5 percent margin of error should follow the standard reporting formats used in national polls. Modeling the *New York Times*/CBS Poll, for example, the margin of error statement might read as follows: In theory, in 19 out of 20 cases, the results based on samples such as this one will differ by no more than 5 percent from what would have been obtained by interviewing all classroom teachers in the school district.

Technically speaking, there are two estimates of interest in our example. First, the 55 percent yes responses is called a *statistic* which is a summary measure for a set of sample responses. This statistic is a *point estimate* because it provides the best single point to estimate the population *parameter*, a summary measure that can be calculated *only* when the requested information is available for *every* member of the population.

In addition to a *point estimate*, a probability sample provides a second estimate called an *interval estimate*. An *interval estimate* indicates a range rather than a single point. This range is used to acknowledge that the information in a sample reflects sampling error regarding the true value of the parameter.

Thinking in terms of our example, the lower bound of the interval estimate is equal to the point estimate minus 5 percent. This difference is 50 percent. Similarly, the upper bound of the interval estimate is equal to 55 percent plus 5 percent or 60 percent. Thus, the range of the interval estimate is twice the value of the margin of error. To verify this is true, one can inspect the difference between the upper bound (60 percent) and the lower bound (50 percent). This difference is 10 percent, a value which is exactly twice the 5 percent margin of error.

For the record, it is of interest to note that the *New York Times*/CBS margin of error statement and the sample percent are all that is needed to construct the interval estimate. Moreover, given the theoretical information about 19 out of 20 cases in this statement, one also knows that the interval estimate represents a 95 percent confidence interval.

Note 2—Every probability sampling design has both a *selection* *process* (the rules by which the actual sample is selected) and a corresponding *estimation process* (the rules by which the sample estimate of the population parameter and its margin of error are determined). For example, Table 1.1 is a selection process table. Table 1.2 is an estimation process table. Similarly, Tables 1.3 and 1.4 are estimation process tables. Tables 1.5 and 1.6 are selection process tables. Table 1.7 is also a selection process table. It offers several selection alternatives for the recommended sample size to be used for the population of 10,000 classroom teachers.

This two-part strategy for probability sampling work is well treated in an easy-to-read basic survey sampling text. See Schaeffer, Mendenhall and Ott (1990). Chapter Four of this source addresses simple random sampling designs, the design used in this article. For a more mathematical source, deemed by most behavioral science survey sampling statisticians to be one of the very best sources for demographers and social science practitioners, see Kish (1965).

Educators may also want to examine Jaeger (1984) to get some basic insights on how survey sampling can be applied effectively to a wide array of typical problems encountered in educational organizations.

Note 3 – Technically speaking, the American Association for Public Opinion Research (AAPOR) has set both ethical guidelines and scientific standards for reporting survey research findings. In addition to reporting the margin of error, there are seven other items that the AAPOR believe must appear in a publication reporting survey results. These are sample size, sponsor, response rate, dates when data were collected, an accurate definition of the population, how respondents were contacted, and the precise wording of questions used in the survey.

An excellent overview of both ethical and scientific consideration to be addressed in conducting and reporting survey findings is given in Chapter 19 of Babbie (1990). See also Chapter 20 of Babbie for an insightful checklist to evaluate all aspects of a published survey.

Note 4 – The procedures for determining the school preference survey margin of error elaborated in Tables 1.3 and 1.4 can be applied to any simple random sampling design where N, n, p, and *A* are available. Accordingly, this procedure can also be used by consumers of research to create an accurate margin of error for any published survey findings.

If *A* is not reported, the consumer can choose his or her own values for the confidence level to be used in constructing the margin of error. Most often, consumers will choose the square root of *A* which is equal to 1.96 to yield the traditional 95 percent confidence interval. This square root value was used in step six of Table 1.3.

Note 5 – Setting *B* equal to 0.08 rather than to 0.05 means the *maximum* margin of error will never exceed eight rather than five percent. However, since the actual sample proportion *p* can range from zero to one, it is quite possible the actual margin of error (with a 95 percent confidence coefficient still in place) will be significantly less than 8 percent.

For example, if the actual survey findings proportion is 0.90 (a 90 percent *yes* response from our teacher sample), the actual margin of error (using Table 1.4 procedures with a sample size of 138) is only 4.8 percent.

Note 6 – Changing just the confidence coefficient will still preserve the preprogrammed value request to keep a maximum bound that is no more than five percent. However, as a result of reducing *A*, the actual bound for the unchanged margin of error has a 90 percent rather than 95 percent confidence coefficient.

Careful examination of the third exploration reveals another interesting feature. The last entry in this exploration is used to increase just the confidence coefficient. Accordingly, A is set at 6.63. This change will also preserve the maximum bound request. It will now yield a 99 percent confidence coefficient. However, this change is not without some cost. Specifically, the increase from 95 to 99 percent confidence requires a corresponding increase in sample size from 370 to 622.

Note 7 – For this proposed sampling design, the actual margin of error will have a 90 percent confidence coefficient and a maximum bound of seven percent. If the survey is implemented and the findings yield an 85 percent *yes* response from the 103 classroom teachers in the random sample, the actual margin of error (using the Table 1.4 procedure with *n* equal to 103 and the square root of *A* set at 1.64) is only 5.7 percent.

Recall also that the binomial distribution is symmetrical. Thus, the margin of error for a 15 percent yes response from classroom teachers would also be 5.7 percent.

This example clearly indicates that a researcher can simultaneously vary either two or three of the preprogrammed decision rules. Also, the explorations undertaken in Step Two of the three-step procedure should provide sufficient evidence to suggest a survey group is never left with just the one sample size solution encountered in published sample size tables such as Krejcie and Morgan (1970).

Note 8 – A stratified random sampling design can be viewed as a series of simple random sampling designs where each person in the population appears on only one list. For an easy-to-read treatment of all essential features of stratified sampling, consult Chapter Five of Schaeffer et al. (1990).

In a policy preference survey of members in each of several stakeholder groups, some names will appear on more than one list. For example, a teacher may also be a parent. This poses no real problem. If a teacher's name is selected from a population list of teachers, the response requested would be from a teacher's perspective. If the teacher's name is also selected from a population list of parents, the parent's viewpoint would be requested.

Note 9 – If the restructuring committee wished to compare the preferences of two or more stakeholder groups using formal statistical tests such as a *t*-test of proportions from two independent groups or an *F-test* of the proportions of two or more independent groups entered in an analysis of variance model, then sample sizes should be based on sample size formulas used in hypothesis testing designs to ensure adequate statistical power. Differences in the decision rules between formulas used here in estimation and those used in hypothesis testing are treated in McNamara (1990).

The specific reason for recommending at least 100 respondents in each stakeholder group is to ensure that the survey sampling design and the corresponding test statistics are able to detect real and meaningful group differences. For a brief overview of statistical power and its sampling requirements, see McNamara (1991).

Note 10 – Excellent ideas for questionnaire items are given in the *Phi Delta Kappan*'s Hot Topics Series on year-round schools assembled by their Center on Evaluation, Development and Research (see Williams, 1990).

Those seriously interested in conducting a school preference survey might wish to examine the following excellent questionnaire design sources. On constructing either telephone or postal questionnaires see Dillman (1979); on designing and conducting questionnaire surveys as a school/ university collaborative venture consult Smith, McNamara and Barona (1986); on reporting findings to policy makers and practitioners examine Haensly, Lupkowski and McNamara (1987) and Borg and Gall (1989, Chapter 21).

Note 11 – In practical survey sampling designs, it is not unusual to preset *P* equal to 0.75 rather than to the traditional preset value of 0.50, even though no reliable prior information is readily available. In my own survey sampling work, I almost always use this rule of thumb when either survey research resources are limited or when there is a very short time allocation for conducting and reporting survey findings.

Technically speaking, this is done for two reasons. First, differences in the two resulting standard errors are almost always very small. For example, if *n* is 370 (as was the case in the initial solution presented in Step 1), the maximum standard errors are 0.022 for *P* (a population parameter) equal to 0.50 and 0.025 for *P* equal to 0.75. Notice the difference cannot be determined until we move to the third digit to the right of the decimal point. Even then the difference is almost trivial.

Second, starting with a preset value of *P* equal to 0.75 rather than 0.50, the required sample size reduction is usually significant. In our case study, the recommended classroom teacher sample size for *P* pretest at 0.50 is 370. However, if we preset *P* at 0.75 for the same case study, the recommended sample size is only 280, a reduction of 90 teachers.

PROBLEMS

Two specific survey research design problems are given here for those who wish to verify that they can use the selection and estimation procedures specified in this chapter. Both problems can be done without reference to other survey research materials. Solutions to these two problems are given in the back of the book.

Problem 1.1

An urban school district wishes to conduct a school preference survey that is identical to the one described in this chapter. Specifically, this school district wishes to design a simple random sample survey to estimate the proportion of its 800 classroom teachers (N) who would give a *yes* response to the single questionnaire item identified in the chapter example.

The survey research design decisions established by the school district are as follows:

1. The precision (B) is preset at 0.05.
2. The confidence coefficient (A) is preset at 3.84.
3. The prior information value (P) is preset at 0.50.

For the record, these preprogrammed decisions are the same three preprogrammed decisions introduced in the chapter discussion of "Step 1: The Initial Solution."

Use the procedure given in Table 1.5 to get the recommended sample size (n) for this preference survey. Your solutions to this problem should be a table that is identical in form to the one given in Table 1.6.

Problem 1.2

Assume that the classroom teacher preference survey was conducted using the required sample size (n) you identified in your solution to Problem 1.1. Also assume that the proportion of *yes* responses in this survey was 0.85 (i.e., 85 percent of the teachers in the sample gave a *yes* response to the questionnaire item on the preference for a year-round school program).

Your task is to determine the margin of error for this school preference survey using the six-step procedure detailed in Table 1.3. Your solution to this problem should be a table that is identical in form to the one given in Table 1.4.

REFERENCES

Babbie, E. 1990. *Survey Research Methods, 2nd Ed.* Belmont: Wadsworth.

Borg, W. A. and M. Gall. 1989. *Educational Research, 5th Ed.* New York: Longman.

Dillman, D. A. 1979. *Mail and Telephone Surveys: The Total Design Method.* New York: Wiley.

Haensly, P. A., A. E. Lupkowski, and J. F. McNamara. 1987. "The Chart Essay: A Strategy for Communicating Research Findings to Policy Makers and Practitioners," *Educational Evaluation and Policy Analysis*, 9(1):63–75.

Jaeger, R. M. 1984. *Sampling in Education and Social Sciences.* New York: Longman.

Kish, L. 1965. *Survey Sampling.* New York: Wiley.

Krejcie, R. V. and D. A. Morgan. 1970. "Determining Sample Size for Research Activities," *Educational and Psychological Measurement*, 30(6):607–610.

McNamara, J. F. 1991. "Statistical Power in Educational Research," *National Forum of Applied Educational Research Journal*, 3(2): 23–26.

McNamara, J. F. 1990. "The Sample Size Issue in Educational Administration," *Record in Educational Administration and Supervision*, 10(2):46–49.

McNamara, J. F. 1978. "Determining Sample Size in Decision-Oriented Research," *Planning and Changing: A Journal for School Administrators*, 9(2):125–127.

Schaeffer, R. L., W. Mendenhall, and L. Ott. 1990. *Elementary Survey Sampling, 4th Ed.* Boston: Duxbury.

Smith, R. G., J. F. McNamara, and A. Barona. 1986. "Getting 'Good' Results from Survey Research," *Public Administration Quarterly*, 10(2):233–248.

Williams, S., ed. 1990. *Year-Round Schools: Do They Make a Difference?* Bloomington: Phi Delta Kappa.

CHAPTER 2

The Effect Size Criterion in School Improvement Research

MOVING beyond technical definitions and elaborate descriptions, it is safe to say that meaningful educational reforms seek to identify new and innovative ways to improve schools. With this common purpose in mind, educational reformers often focus their search efforts on one or more specific shared goals such as improving teaching and learning, increasing the high school graduation rates, reducing school discipline problems, and extending parent involvement in school decision making.

It is important to note that there is no one best way to structure all of the specific activities reformers can use to conduct a school improvement search. However, most would agree that a productive search requires a reform group to complete three general tasks.

Put briefly, these tasks are (1) locating an alternative strategy that is likely to be more effective than the current practice, (2) conducting a fair test that compares the effectiveness of both strategies, and (3) using the comparative test results to reevaluate the belief regarding the increased effectiveness of the alternative strategy.

When the outcome measure used in a school improvement search is a continuous variable (means or percents and their standard deviations can be determined), the traditional method used to compare the effectiveness of two different strategies is the t test for two independent samples. In this test model, the criterion used to recognize a differential effect is the presence or absence of a statistically significant difference.

This chapter introduces an alternative method that reformers can use to compare the effectiveness of two different strategies. The alternative method uses an effect size rather than a statistical significance criterion to guide decisions regarding the detection of differential effects.

The intent of this article is to elaborate several advantages for using the effect size criterion approach. Theoretically speaking, the effect size approach is advocated by many modern behavioral science statisticians (Cohen, 1988 and Shavelson, 1988) and research design specialists (Borg, 1988; Borg and Gall, 1989; and Shaver, 1991).

Practically speaking, the effect size approach has three distinct advantages. First, it provides a straightforward way for practitioners to accurately define meaningful differences in their own terms without reference to statistical significance. Second, this alternative approach uses exactly the same basic data used in t test models. Thus, no new data are required. Third, neither analysis of data nor reporting of results depends on having an in-depth knowledge of inferential statistics. Accordingly, effect size findings can be understood and easily communicated by policy makers and practitioners responsible for implementing school improvement decisions.

Using a single school improvement case study to focus the discussion, these advantages are elaborated in the responses to these four specific questions:

1. How is the statistical significance criterion used to detect differential effects?
2. Does statistical significance automatically imply that meaningful differences have been detected?
3. How can the effect size criterion be used to detect meaningful differences?
4. How can the effect size criterion approach be used to explain meaningful differences to policy makers and practitioners without reference to technical statistical terms used in estimation theory and hypothesis testing?

With this in mind, the chapter is divided into four parts, each part providing an answer to one of these questions. In addition, the case study is introduced in the first part and used throughout the chapter to clarify the answers provided for each of the four specific questions elaborated above.

STATISTICAL SIGNIFICANCE

Following the recommendations reported in the new National Council of Teachers of Mathematics standards for improving mathematics in elementary and secondary schools (Ball and Schroeder, 1992), a large urban school district decided that one of the primary goals it wished to pursue was improving student performance in senior high school mathematics. Accordingly, a district task force was formed to investigate how this might be done.

After conducting an intensive fact-finding effort, the task force decided its first goal should be to improve teaching and learning in its Algebra I classes. They believed that this initial goal was an essential first step and one likely to directly influence future efforts to improve more advanced mathematics courses offered in the district.

With this shared goal in mind, the district's task force is in an excellent position to undertake a school improvement search.

The first task for this action research group would be to locate a more effective strategy for teaching Algebra I courses. Let us assume that this task has been completed and the district's task force is convinced that teaching Algebra I using the problem solving and graphic method (Kysh, 1991) will increase student achievement in Algebra I (see Note 1).

The second task for this action research group would be to conduct a fair test that compares the performance of the district's Algebra I students exposed to the new experimental teaching method with those who are taught Algebra I using the traditional method (the method used in prior years). The typical length of time for a valid comparative experiment such as this one would be a single school year (see Note 2).

The third task for this group would be to evaluate the results of the district's experiment. A careful evaluation of student performance results would clearly support (or fail to support) the task force's belief that the new method of teaching Algebra I is more effective in their school district. Depending on the actual experimental outcomes, the task force could recommend (or not recommend) that the school district adopt the new method in all Algebra I classes (see Note 3).

The Logic of Hypothesis Testing

An overview of how this comparative experiment would proceed is given in Table 2.1. Notice that the experiment is guided by a single research hypothesis. For the record, it should be stated that research hypotheses are theoretical statements (informed conjectures or educated guesses) about an expected difference or an expected relationship. They are not statistical statements, and they do not need to be put in null form.

In this case study, the research hypothesis is a directional hypothesis. Its direction reflects the task force's belief that the alternative (new) teaching method will be more effective for their students.

The district's fair test experiment begins with a random selection of students from the district's entire population of Algebra I students. Next, the sample of students chosen to participate in the experiment is randomly assigned to either Method One (the new experimental teaching alternative) or Method Two (the traditional teaching strategy).

These sampling procedures are used to avoid any problems that might result from using a biased sample. For example, if academically advanced or above grade students were assigned only to Method One, the experiment is no longer a fair test (see Note 4).

To achieve a fair test, several environmental and classroom factors would need to be controlled. For example, equally competent teachers should be assigned to each method to avoid teacher assignment bias. Algebra I classes for both groups in the experiment should be scheduled for the same periods. Most important,

Table 2.1. The Algebra I experimental study.

Research Hypothesis: The experimental method (#1) is more effective than the traditional method (#2).

Verification Strategy: Design and conduct a true experiment to verify the claim made in the research hypothesis.

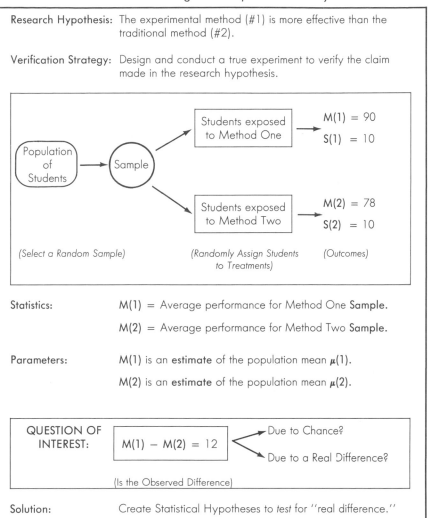

	(Select a Random Sample)

Statistics: M(1) = Average performance for Method One **Sample.**

M(2) = Average performance for Method Two **Sample.**

Parameters: M(1) is an **estimate** of the population mean $\mu(1)$.

M(2) is an **estimate** of the population mean $\mu(2)$.

QUESTION OF
INTEREST: M(1) − M(2) = 12   Due to Chance?
                                     Due to a Real Difference?

(Is the Observed Difference)

Solution: Create Statistical Hypotheses to *test* for "real difference."

the two teaching methods should be monitored to ensure that both methods were implemented according to the guidelines and strategies required for that method (see Note 5).

The experimental results for this case study are entered in Table 2.1. This outcome measure reflects a summary of results (means and standard deviations) for the two sample groups on a standardized Algebra I examination known to have an excellent content validity in terms of the district's Algebra I curriculum guide.

Since the Table 2.1 results were obtained from two experimental samples, they are called statistics. For example, the sample mean $M(1)$ is a statistic because it is a summary measure based on all the Algebra I test scores for students in the experiment exposed to Method One. As a statistic, $M(1)$ is an unbiased estimate for $\mu(1)$, a parameter reflecting what the mean would have been if the entire school district Algebra I student population were taught using only Method One.

Similarly, $M(2)$ is also a statistic. It provides an estimate for $\mu(2)$, a second parameter of interest that reflects the typical student performance when only Method Two is used throughout the district.

Hence, $\mu(1)$ and $\mu(2)$ are parameters that reflect two different policy options available to the school district. From a policy research perspective, the fair-test experiment is a practical one because it models exactly the two actual policy options under investigation by the district's task force.

The big question to be addressed in the inferential model elaborated in Table 2.1 is to determine if the observed sample mean difference of 12 points is more likely to be due to chance (happened only because of sampling error) or due to real difference (one method is actually more effective).

It is at this point in the analysis of experimental data that one becomes interested in statistical hypotheses and statistical significance. Specifically, in the logic of hypothesis testing, statistical hypotheses and probability theory can be used to help the decision maker reach an informed decision about the actual sample mean difference encountered in the experiment.

Statistical Hypotheses

While research hypotheses are theoretical and are expressed verbally using concepts, statistical hypotheses are empirical and are expressed in terms of parameters.

The traditional statistical model used to test whether the sample mean difference of 12 is due to chance or due to a real difference is the t test for two independent samples. Application of this traditional testing model is elaborated in Table 2.2.

In step one the researcher formulates two statistical hypotheses. The null hypothesis labeled **H(0)** in Table 2.2 equates $\mu(1)$ to $\mu(2)$. This null hypothesis suggests that the two parameters are equal, implying that any observed difference in the two sample means is due only to chance. Thus, the null statistical hypothesis for this experiment places the two parameters in an equation to infer that the two treatments are equally effective (see Note 6).

Since **H(0)** might not be true, one needs to specify an alternative statistical hypothesis which must be true if **H(0)** is false. Accordingly, step one in Table 2.2 specifies **H(A)**, an alternative statistical hypothesis which fits this logical requirement.

Put another way, either **H(0)** is true and there is no differential effect, or **H(A)** is true and a differential effect is inferred. Hence, **H(0)** and **H(A)** are complementary, which implies that they have no overlap and between them they exhaust all possible outcomes of the experiment.

Statistical Decision Rules

The second step in applying the traditional t test model requires the researcher to specify a decision rule for rejecting **H(0)**. Statistical decision rules are based on probability and the actual sample sizes in the two independent groups.

For this school district case study, let us make two assumptions to get started. First, assume that the t test procedure will use a significance level (or alpha value) equal to 0.05. This specification indicates that there is a 5 percent error rate and a corresponding 95 percent confidence in the findings of the t test. Second, assume that the two samples are equal and there are twenty-five students in each group (see Note 7).

The correct step two decision rules for the above specifics are given in Table 2.2. The null hypothesis would be rejected if the t test value for the experimental findings from Table 2.1 was greater than 2.02, a theoretical value from the t distribution for a total sample size of fifty (see Note 8).

In step three the t test value for the experimental data is

Table 2.2. Application of the t test for the Algebra I experiment.

Step One: Indicate the statistical hypotheses

    Null Hypothesis   H(0): $\mu(1)$ equals $\mu(2)$
    Alternative Hypothesis   H(A): $\mu(1)$ is not equal to $\mu(2)$

    H(0) is a statistical null hypothesis indicating that the two methods of teaching Algebra I are equally effective.

    H(A) is a statistical alternative hypothesis indicating that the two methods of teaching Algebra I are *not* equally effective.

    $\mu(1)$ is a parameter indicating the mean performance score for the district's Algebra I student population when all students are taught using Method One.

    $\mu(2)$ is a parameter indicating the mean performance score for the district's Algebra I student population when all students are taught using Method Two.

Step Two: Specify the decision rules for evaluating H(0)

    For an experimental test group having 25 students in each sample and a significance level (alpha) set at 0.05, the two decision rules are:

    Reject H(0) if the t test value observed exceeds **2.02**

    Retain H(0) if the t test value observed does *not* exceed **2.02**

Step Three: Calculate the t test statistic for the experiment

    The essential input information needed to apply the t test for two independent samples is

    • Sample size for Method One is **25**
    • Sample size for Method Two is **25**
    • Sample mean difference is **12**
    • Common standard deviation is **10**

    Inserting this information into the t test formula, the observed t test value for this experiment is **4.24**

Step Four: Indicate the decision regarding H(0)

    The observed t test value of **4.24** exceeds the decision rule t test value of **2.02** specified in step two above. Thus, H(0) is rejected and a statistically significant difference favoring Method One is detected.

Step Five: Interpret the t test findings

    Given a statistically significant difference favoring Method One, the researcher would conclude that Method One was a more effective method for teaching Algebra I in the district where the experiment was conducted.

---

calculated. For a sample mean difference of twelve, two identical standard deviations of ten, and two equal sample sizes of twenty-five each, the actual t test value is 4.24 (see Note 9).

In step four the decision rule is linked with the actual t test value to reach a decision regarding H(0). From Table 2.2 one can see that the actual t test value of 4.24 is greater than the critical t test value of 2.02 specified in the decision rule. Accordingly, the researcher would reject H(0) and indicate that a statistically significant difference was detected.

Step Five in the traditional t test model is used to draw a conclusion about the research hypothesis. Using the statistical significance criterion, the researcher would conclude in this case study that Method One was a more effective strategy for teaching Algebra I.

It is important to recognize that this conclusion follows in the traditional analysis only because a statistically significant difference was uncovered. Had no statistically significant difference been uncovered, the researcher would have concluded that the two teaching methods were equally effective.

STATISTICAL SIGNIFICANCE AND MEANINGFUL DIFFERENCES

When the standard technique for testing the hypothesis of the difference between two independent sample means merely involves selecting a level of significance (alpha) and setting the corresponding critical t test value for accepting or rejecting the null statistical hypothesis, only half the story of hypothesis testing has been told. The other half of the story requires one to determine if the statistical significance relfects a trivial or a meaningful difference.

Thinking in terms of the school district case study elaborated above, it is important to recognize that the statistically significant difference uncovered in step four of the traditional t test model presented in Table 2.2 is an extremely poor measure of an experimental outcome. This is true because the probability level associated with the observed t test value reported in step four of Table 2.2 is a function of sample size.

Put briefly, the problem is as follows: since sample size directly influences the calculation of a t test value, trivial as well as meaningful differences can be statistically significant.

The Sample Size Problem

While it is seldom recognized and almost never explored in practice, the actual influence of sample size on the traditional t test is easy to demonstrate. This can be seen clearly by increasing the sample sizes for the two groups in the case study experiment. This has been done in Table 2.3.

The first column in Table 2.3 is used to simulate an increase in the sample sizes for the two groups. The first entry in this column is twenty-five students per group. This entry represents the actual sample sizes used to construct the hypothesis testing model presented in Table 2.2. Additional entries in this column allow the sample size to increase from this initial value of twenty-five students per group to a final value of 6,400 students per group.

The second column of Table 2.3 provides the critical t test value used in the decision rule for rejecting **H(0)**. The first entry in this column is 2.02. This is the same critical t test value used in step

Table 2.3. Mean difference requirements for statistical significance.

Sample Size	Critical t Value	Required Mean Difference
25	2.02	5.71
50	2.00	4.00
100	1.96	2.77
200	1.96	1.96
400	1.96	1.39
800	1.96	0.98
1,600	1.96	0.69
6,400	1.96	0.35

Note: Critical t values are based on a t test model that uses a 0.05 significance level and a two-tailed test. The first entry in Table 2.3 can be interpreted as follows. Given 25 students in each of two independent samples, a critical t test value greater than **2.02** is needed to infer that a statistically significant difference has been detected. A required mean difference provides an equivalent decision rule for the same t test situation. Accordingly, an observed mean difference greater than **5.71** is needed to infer a statistically significant difference when there are 25 students in each sample.

two of Table 2.2. The decision rule indicates that a statistically significant difference is to be acknowledged if the observed t test value exceeds 2.02.

The last column of Table 2.3 provides an equivalent decision rule for rejecting H(0). This decision rule indicates that a critical t test value of 2.02 is identical to a sample mean difference of 5.71. This equivalent decision rule is exactly what is needed to explore the influence of sample size on the requirements for statistical significance (see Note 10).

For example, if the number of students in each group is increased to 100, the critical t test value for rejecting H(0) is 1.96. Using the equivalent rule for this fourfold increase in both sample sizes, a statistically significant difference will be declared if the observed sample mean difference between M(1) and M(2) is greater than 2.77.

Increasing the sample size again by a factor of four increases the sample size to 400 students in each experimental group. While the critical t test value for this sampling plan remains at 1.96, the required sample mean difference to acknowledge statistical significance is reduced to 1.39.

Finally, when there are 1,600 students in each experimental group used in the case study—a sampling plan that is well within the realm of possibility for a large urban school district with several senior high schools—the observed sample mean difference needed for statistical significance is only 0.69.

Thus, one can see from the Table 2.3 illustration that increasing the sample sizes from twenty-five students to 1,600 students per group results in decreasing the required mean difference for statistical significance from 5.71 to 0.69.

This direct influence of sample size on statistical significance can also be expressed as a ratio. Put briefly, the sample mean difference of 5.71 needed for statistical significance when there are twenty-five students per group is eight times the size of the required sample mean difference of 0.69 needed to acknowledge statistical significance when 1,600 students are placed in each group.

In a word, what this Table 2.3 illustration clearly demonstrates is the following: reliance on just the traditional t test procedure lets a single statistical formula, directly influenced by sample size, dictate whether or not a meaningful difference has been uncovered in the comparative experiment.

While not recommended as a general rule, this Table 2.3 information on the influence of sample size reveals an obvious strategy. If reformers wish to use statistical significance as the sole criterion to justify a differential effect, they should always use very large samples in their comparative experiments. This strategy is almost always guaranteed to yield statistically significant results (see Note 11).

EFFECT SIZE CRITERION

The solution to difficulties posed by sample size is straightforward. What is needed is a statistical decision rule for detecting a meaningful difference that is not influenced by sample size. The effect size criterion is a decision rule that meets this need.

An effect size is a statistical construct that takes the form of a *ratio*. When two sample groups are compared, the effect size numerator is the observed sample mean difference. The corresponding effect size denominator is the common standard deviation for the two sample groups.

The effect size allows one to express observed sample mean differences in standard deviation units. As we shall soon see, differences expressed in standard deviation units allow an effect size indicator to be interpreted using a normal distribution.

Two properties of effect size deserve mention at this point. First, an effect size value of zero implies that the outcome measure for a typical student in one group is no different than the typical score for a student in the other group. Obviously, this situation can occur only when the two sample means are equal.

Second, the larger the effect size value, the larger the differential effect favoring the group with the higher sample mean. Moreover, the larger the effect size, the more likely it is that the observed difference is a meaningful difference.

The calculation and interpretation of the effect size as a criterion to detect meaningful differences can be illustrated using the Algebra I case study data from Table 2.1.

Calculating Effect Sizes

The effect size numerator is the difference between the two sample means. This is **M(1)**, which equals 90, minus **M(2)**, which equals 72. This subtraction yields a sample mean difference equal to twelve points on the Algebra I test. the observed difference of twelve points favors the students taught by the new teaching alternative.

Table 2.4 provides a step-by-step procedure required to get the common standard deviation. This procedure will work for either equal or unequal sample sizes.

Table 2.5 applies this procedure to yield a common standard deviation of ten for the Algebra I experiment. Given the two standard deviations were equal, this result should not surprise us.

Table 2.6 is used to put the numerator and denominator results together to yield an effect size value for the Algebra I case study experiment equal to 1.2.

Table 2.4. Extimating a common standard deviation.

Step One:	Calculate A = N(1) minus One.
Step Two:	Evaluate B = the product of A and V(1).
Step Three:	Calculate C = N(2) minus One.
Step Four:	Evaluate D = the product of C and V(2).
Step Five:	Specify E = the sum of B and D.
Step Six:	Specify F = the sum of A and C.
Step Seven:	Determine G = E divided by F.
Step Eight:	Evaluate H = the square root of G.

N(1) = the sample size for sample one.
V(1) = the variance for sample one.
N(2) = the sample size for sample two.
V(2) = the variance for sample two.
A = the degrees of freedom for sample one.
B = the sum of squares for sample one.
C = the degrees of freedom for sample two.
D = the sum of squares for sample two.
E = the total sum of squares due to sampling error.
F = the total degrees of freedom for the *t* test.
G = the common variance.
H = the common standard deviation.

Table 2.5. Calculating a common standard deviation.

Step One:	A = 25 − 1 = 24
Step Two:	B = (24) (100) = 2,400
Step Three:	C = 25 − 1 = 24
Step Four:	D = (24) (100) = 2,400
Step Five:	E = 2,400 + 2,400 = 4,800
Step Six:	F = 24 + 24 = 48
Step Seven:	G = 4,800 divided by 48 = 100
Step Eight:	H = Square root of 100 = 10

Note: This procedure can be used for either equal or unequal sample sizes for the two independent groups. In a traditional t test for two independent samples, H is called the pooled standard deviation. In a oneway analysis of variance with two groups, E is the within group sum of squares, F is the within group degrees of freedom and G is the within group mean square which is the denominator in the F test ratio. Thus, the common standard deviation H is the square root of the within group mean square found in an F test table.

Table 2.6. Calculating and interpreting effect sizes.

Formula

ES = SMD divided by CSD
ES = 12 divided by 10 = 1.2

Legend

ES = the effect size estimate.
SMD = the sample mean differences.
CSD = the common standard deviation.

Interpretation

Given the Algebra I experiment having a 12 point sample mean difference favoring students taught by Method One, and a common standard deviation equal to 10 points, the effect size estimate is 1.2. this effect size estimate has the following interpretation:

On average,
    students taught by Method One
      have performance scores
        that are 1.2 standard deviations higher
      than the performance scores
        for student taught by Method Two.

Interpreting Effect Sizes

Statistically speaking, an effect size value of 1.2 can be interpreted as follows: the typical Algebra I student taught by Method One had an achievement score that was 1.2 standard deviations higher than the achievement score of a typical student taught by Method Two.

Practically speaking, one can say that an effect size of 1.2 is an extremely meaningful difference. It can be summarized as follows: an additional 38 percent of the students had higher Algebra I test scores when taught by Method One rather than Method Two.

This 38 percent advantage can be explained by studying the effect size profiles offered in Table 2.7. This explanation begins by locating an effect size of 1.2 in the first column of Table 2.7. Using the outcome information from the Algebra I experi-

Table 2.7. Using the normal distribution to interpret effect sizes.

Effect Size	Method Two Group (% above M(2) = 78)	Method One Group (% above M(2) = 78)	Difference (%)
0.00	50.0	50.0	0
0.10	50.0	54.0	4
0.20	50.0	58.0	8
0.30	50.0	62.0	12
0.40	50.0	65.0	15
0.50	50.0	69.0	19
0.60	50.0	73.0	23
0.80	50.0	79.0	29
1.00	50.0	84.0	34
1.20	50.0	88.0	38
1.50	50.0	93.0	43
2.00	50.0	98.0	48

Note: M(2) is the sample mean for the Method Two Group. It is the *smaller* of the two sample means. With this in mind, entries in Table 2.7 can be interpreted as follows. An effect size of 0.50 (see row six) tells us that the students in the Method One group on average scored a half standard deviation higher than the students in the Method Two Group. While 50 percent of the Method Two students had scores above their sample mean score of 78 (see column two), 69 percent of the Method One students had scores above the sample two mean score of 78 (see column three). Thus, an effect size of 0.50 implies that an additional 19 percent of students will have higher test scores when taught by Method One rather than Method Two. This 19 percent advantage is entered in column four. Other table entries can be interpreted in an identical manner. While this illustration was developed using the Algebra I case study, the advantage percent interpretation offered here can be used to interpret the effect size results for any t test involving two independent samples.

ment, the second column entry for this effect size indicates that 50 percent of the students taught by Method Two had performance scores above the sample two mean of 78.

The third column also uses the sample two mean of 78 as a reference point. Knowing that the Method One test scores were 1.2 standard deviations higher tells us that 88 percent of the students taught by Method One exceeded the sample two mean score of 78.

The 88 percent entry in column three has a straightforward explanation. Given a normal curve with a mean of 78 and a standard deviation of 10, a score of 90, which is the sample mean for Method One, is located at the 88th percentile (see Note 12). The final column in Table 2.7 gives the difference for the two previous entries. For an effect size of 1.2, this difference is 88 percent minus 50 percent or 38 percent (see Note 13).

Effect Sizes as Decision Rules

Four specific properties make an effect size an excellent statistical decision rule to use in hypothesis testing.

First, further examination of Table 2.7 tells us that any effect size can be linked to a specific advantage expressed as a percent favoring the higher of two independent sample means.

For example, an effect size of 0.3 yields a 12 percent advantage. Similarly, an effect size of 0.8 yields a 29 percent advantage to the group having a higher sample mean. Other Table 2.7 values can be interpreted in the same manner.

Second, an effect size indicator is not dependent on knowing the sample sizes used in an experiment. Thus, an effect size of interest can be specified long before an actual experiment is conducted.

Third, since effect size calculations are not based on sample sizes, increasing sample sizes in an experiment will not reduce the value needed to achieve a meaningful difference.

Fourth, and most important, effect sizes provide individual researchers or action research groups a concrete means to define a meaningful difference that meets their specific needs (see Note 14).

With these four properties in mind, those wishing to detect

meaningful differential results should consider replacing the critical t test decision rule used in the traditional t test model with one expressed in terms of an effect size of interest. Using the effect size criterion is easy. It would work as follows in the Algebra I experiment. Assume the district task force in our case study believed a 19 percent advantage for Method One (the new alternative teaching method uncovered in the initial stage of their school improvement search) would be sufficient for them to acknowledge a differential effect and recommend that the school district adopt Method One.

The traditional step two decision rule in the Table 2.2 hypothesis testing model elaboration would now read as follows: Reject H(0) if the observed effect size equals or exceeds 0.5. The complementary decision rule would read as follows: Retain H(0) if the observed effect size is less than 0.5.

As we know from the information provided earlier in Table 2.6 where the actual effect size estimate was 1.2, H(0) would be rejected. With these results in hand (a 38 percent advantage for students taught by Method One rather than Method Two), the district task force would be in an excellent position to recommend that the new alternative method be adopted throughout the district.

What also deserves mention here is the fact that every member of the district's task force should be able to calculate and interpret the effect size for themselves without reference to technical statistical formulas or complex inferential rules.

SCHOOL IMPROVEMENT SEARCHES

There are three different opportunities to use effect size estimates in a school improvement search. These three opportunities can be illustrated using the school district case study.

Using Effect Sizes to Interpret Prior Research

The first task in the school improvement search case study was dedicated to locating a new teaching alternative likely to improve student performance in Algebra I. Prior research studies uncovered in this initial task can be evaluated using effect sizes. These evaluations provide the district's task force with realistic estimates of the Algebra I achievement score gains that the district's students are likely to experience using the new Algebra I teaching method.

An elaboration in Table 2.8 is used to illustrate how this can be done using the findings of a single prior research study. If the school district in this prior research study had a student population similar to the one in the case study district, the Table 2.8 findings suggest that the new method proposed by the district's task force (Method One) is likely to have a 21 percent advantage over the current teaching method (Method Two).

If several appropriate prior research studies were uncovered by the district's task force, effect size estimates for each of these studies can be determined using the Table 2.8 procedure. Next, these effect sizes can be combined to get an overall advantage

Table 2.8. Using an effect size to evaluate prior research.

Method One Data	Method Two Data
Sample Mean = 87 Standard Deviation = 14 Sample Variance = 196 Sample Size = 60	Sample Mean = 80 Standard Deviation = 10 Sample Variance = 100 Sample Size = 40
Common Standard Deviation	
Step One: Step Two: Step Three: Step Four: Step Five: Step Six: Step Seven: Step Eight:	A = 60 − 1 = 59 B = 59 (196) = 11,564 C = 40 − 1 = 39 D = 39 (100) = 3.900 E = 11,564 + 3,900 = 15,464 F = 59 + 39 = 98 G = 157.76 H = 12.56
Effect Size	
ES = SMD divided by CSD = 7.0 divided by 12.56 = 0.56	
Interpretation	
An effect size estimate of **0.56** implies that an additional **21** percent of students will have higher test scores when taught by Method One rather than Method Two.	

percent. In educational research terms, this quantitative synthesis strategy is called meta-analysis (see Note 15).

Using Effect Sizes to Define Meaningful Differences

The second task in a school improvement search is used to conduct a fair test experiment that compares a proposed new method to a method already in use. The actual design of this fair test experiment should include the specification of a minimum effect size value required for the adoption of the new method.

Thinking again in terms of the case study, the second task in this school improvement search was used to conduct a fair test experiment that compared Method One (the new Algebra I teaching method) to Method Two (the Algebra I teaching method used in prior years). In this search, a minimum effect size of 0.50 was specified as the decision rule that guided the district's task force.

This task two decision rule (specified prior to conducting the fair test experiment) acknowledged that the case study district would be willing to adopt the new Algebra I teaching method in all senior high schools if the fair test experiment had an actual effect size equal to or greater than 0.50 favoring Method One.

An examination of Table 2.7 suggests that declaring an effect size of 0.50 means the district would invest in Method One if it demonstrated that an additional 19 percent (or more) of its Algebra I students had better performance scores when taught by Method One rather than Method Two. Identifying the task two effect size before the fair test experiment is undertaken has three advantages.

First, this effect size decision rule provides district trustees and practitioners with a specific policy statement to guide their school improvement search. As in all strategic planning, there is no replacement for a common expectation known to all stakeholders.

Second, the task two effect size value can be determined using a cost effectiveness perspective that links student performance gains with the additional investment required to implement the new method. In this way, both the desirable and feasible aspects of a school improvement search are addressed explicitly.

Third, this preexperimental effect size specification avoids the problems discussed earlier when only statistical significance is used as the decision rule to acknowledge a meaningful difference.

Using Effect Sizes to Evaluate Experimental Results

The third task in the school improvement search case study was used to reevaluate the task force's belief (research hypothesis) regarding the increased effectiveness of the alternative strategy for teaching Algebra I (Method One).

In this final task, the results of the fair test experiment were expressed as an effect size using the district's actual experimental outcomes. This task three effect size was calculated and interpreted in Table 2.6.

Since the actual experimental effect size of 1.2 was larger than the decision rule effect size of 0.50, the district's task force recommended that Method One be adopted in all district senior high schools.

Using the effect size approach to report the results of the fair test experiment does not require the task force to reference technical statistical terms used in estimation theory and hypothesis testing.

All that needs to be communicated to anyone interested in the outcome of the experiment is this straightforward statement: An effect size value of 1.2 tells us that an additional 38 percent of the district's Algebra I students had better achievement test scores when taught by the new teaching method rather than the teaching method used in previous school years.

SUMMARY

When the outcome measure in a school improvement search is a continuous variable (means or percents and their standard deviations can be determined), the traditional method used to compare the effectiveness of two different strategies is the t test for two independent samples.

This article introduced an alternative method that school improvement researchers can use to compare the effectiveness of two different strategies. The alternative method uses an effect size criterion rather than a statistical significance criterion to guide decisions regarding both the definition and the detection of meaningful differences.

A single school district case study was used to illustrate both the statistical and the practical advantages of using the effect size criterion. *Statistically speaking,* the effect size approach has three clear advantages.

First, the effect size criterion provides a straightforward way to distinguish between statistically significant differences that are trivial and statistically significant differences that are meaningful.

Second, if an effect size criterion is used to specify a meaningful difference before a comparative experiment is conducted, researchers can use this information to determine efficient sample sizes that meet the statistical power requirements for the experiment.

Third, the effect size criterion approach uses exactly the same basic inferential data used in the traditional t test model. Thus, no new data are required to use this alternative approach.

Practically speaking, the effect size criterion approach has four specific advantages for those involved in school improvement research studies.

First, the effect size criterion approach provides an easy way for practitioners and policy makers to accurately define meaningful differences in their own terms without any reference to statistical significance.

Second, the effect size value of interest to policy makers and practitioners can be specified before a comparative experiment is conducted. This specification provides a common expectation for all stakeholders having an interest in the outcomes of a school improvement research project.

Third, a preexperiment effect size value can be determined using a cost effectiveness perspective that links student performance gains with the additional investment required to implement the new method if it proves to be more effective in the experimental test. In this way, both the desirable and feasible aspects of a school improvement search are addressed explicitly before the comparative experiment is undertaken.

Finally, neither analysis of data nor reporting of experimental results depends on an indepth knowledge of inferential statistics. Accordingly, effect size findings can be understood and easily communicated by policy makers and practitioners responsible for implementing school improvement decisions.

Since these advantages are achieved without the loss of either statistical validity or accuracy, the effect size criterion approach should be used by school improvement research groups whenever the opportunity arises to compare the effectiveness of two difference strategies.

NOTES

Throughout the text, references to notes are inserted. The text can be read without reference to these notes. Their purpose is threefold: to extend the information provided on theoretical concepts, to identify a few noteworthy sources on the logic of hypothesis testing, and to specify a few guidelines for readers who may wish to conduct a school improvement search.

Note 1—The task one search undertaken by the district's task force would probably take about four to six months. Several activities would be included in the search to locate an appropriate alternative teaching strategy. Specifically, a review of the mathematics education literature on teaching Algebra I would be conducted by the task force or a mathematics education researcher could be commissioned by the district to generate this review for them.

An active task force would also plan to attend state and national workshops focusing on new and innovative ways to teach senior high school mathematics, attend professional mathematics education conferences to get new insights, and interview "top-of-the-line" mathematics teachers in their region to get additional ideas on how the task force might proceed.

Toward the end of the search when one or two alternative

teaching methods of interest are specified, the task force would probably visit one or more urban school districts (similar to their own) who have had success using these alternative teaching methods. Typically, such visits are very informative and often yield information a task force is unlikely to uncover in the other activities noted above.

Note 2 – To maximize the benefits of a fair-test experiment, a longer rather than a shorter time should be devoted to the experiment. Typically, a valid comparative experiment should span an entire school year. This strategy will allow the task force to observe most consequences likely to occur when a large-scale change is introduced in a district.

Such changes would include extensive inservice training of mathematics teachers. It might also require the district to rethink the content validity of its existing standardized or criterion referenced test for Algebra I. Finally, a large-scale change might require new textbooks and instructional materials. This requirement could be extremely expensive, particularly if the Algebra I texts are new and still have a shelf life of three or four years before they are to be replaced.

Note 3 – It is important to remember that the experiment may *not* yield the expected results the task force had in mind. Even though the literature suggests the new alternative teaching method is more effective, and this method worked in urban districts with characteristics similar to the case study district, there is no absolute guarantee that the new teaching strategy will automatically work in a specific district. Thus, at the close of the experiment, the task force must be prepared to recommend or *not* recommend the new alternative teaching strategy.

Note 4 – If a district does not wish to randomly assign individual students to experimental classes, a requirement for a true experiment, they can assign classes to the two teaching methods. Random assignment of classes rather than individual students is called a quasi-experimental design.

The quasi-experimental design option is frequently used in educational research. An excellent, but nontechnical treatment of quasi-experimental designs is given in Borg and Gall (1989). Additional insights and practical tips on this design are also given in Isaac and Michael (1981).

Note 5 – Excellent guidelines and examples for how to design true experiments in behavioral science studies can be found in Christensen (1988), Mitchell and Jolley (1988) and Fraenkel and Wallen (1990).

Note 6 – Technically speaking, the statistical null hypothesis is a falsification constructed so that the laws of probability can be applied to answer the question raised in Table 2.1. Hence, we do not believe the null hypothesis is true. We use it solely as a means to disconfirm our research hypothesis.

Rejecting **H(0)** allows us to say that the evidence of the experiment is more likely to be consistent with the expected difference specified in the research hypothesis than it is with the counter-position specified in the null hypothesis.

On the need and heuristic value of falsification, one can read almost any philosophy of science text. An excellent but brief overview on the norms of scientific activity can be found in Part One of Babbie (1990). See especially his treatment of disconfirmability of theories which requires the researcher to specify the conditions under which a theoretical statement (research hypothesis) would be disproved.

Note 7 – Setting alpha at 0.05 implies that there is only a five percent chance one will incorrectly reject a true **H(0)**. A second, and equally important error not addressed in the traditional t test model is the possibility one might incorrectly fail to reject a false **H(0)**. The probability of this second error is called beta and its complement (1-beta) is called statistical power.

Description of these two inferential errors and how a researcher should deal with them can be found in most basic statistics texts. For a brief overview of these concerns as they influence the t test for two independent samples see McNamara (1991). An excellent graphic perspective on how these two errors influence statistical power is given in Shavelson (1988, Chapter 12).

Note 8 – Guidelines for the specification of a critical t test value are treated in the hypothesis testing section of a basic statistics text. Two excellent sources one might consult are Shavelson (1988, Chapter 13) and Popham and Sirotnik (1992, Chapters 9 and 10).

For the Algebra I example in Table 2.2, the degrees of freedom indicator needed to use the critical value t test table is equal to the total sample size minus 2. This value is 50 minus 2 which equals 48. Also needed is a value for alpha which is 0.05 and an understanding that a two-tailed test will be used because H(A) is nondirectional. Using this information and the t test table, the correct critical value of t is 2.02.

Note 9 – Excellent step-by-step procedures for calculating and interpreting observed t test values are given in the two sources referenced in Note 8. However, any basic statistics text can be consulted.

For the Algebra I example in Table 2.2, the observed t test value determined in step four is calculated as follows. The numerator of the observed t test value equals the difference between the two sample means. This difference is 12. The corresponding denominator is the standard error of the difference between the two sample means (**SE**). For two equal samples of size 25 each, the value of (**SE**) is 2.828 (see Note 10 for calculations). The observed t test value is 12 divided by 2.828 which equals 4.24, the value entered in step three in Table 2.2.

Note 10 – The equivalent decision rules in Table 2.3 were determined by solving the basic t test formula for the difference between the two sample means. The appropriate critical t test value is used as the t value in this new equation to determine the required sample mean difference for significance.

Since the strategy for specifying the equivalent decision rules used in Table 2.3 is almost never presented in basic statistics texts, a brief overview is given here. The required sample mean difference (**D**) is equal to the product of the critical t test value (**T**) and the standard error for the difference of two independent sample means (**SE**).

When the two independent sample means are equal, **SE** is the square root of the sum of the two sample variances **V(1)** and **V(2)** divided by the common sample size **N**. On this point see Shavelson (1988, page 334).

The equivalent decision rule entered in row one of Table 2.3 was determined as follows. Both **V(1)** and **V(2)** are 100, **T** is 2.02 and **N** is 25. For these values, **SE** equals the square root of (200 divided by 25) which is 2.828. **D** equals the product of 2.828 and 2.02 which is 5.71, the value inserted in Table 2.3.

For **N** equals 1,600, **T** is 1.96 and both **V(1)** and **V(2)** are 100. In this research design, **SE** is the square root of (200 divided by 1,600) which is 0.354. **D** equals the product of 0.354 and 1.96 which is 0.69, the required mean difference needed to reject **H(0)**. Other entries in Table 2.3 can be determined in the same manner using the appropriate value of **N**.

Note 11 – While statistical significance is almost a certainty for extremely large sample sizes, keep in mind that the statistically significant difference uncovered could be trivial and, more important, could favor either the first or second group used in the comparative experiment.

For the record, there is no problem using large samples if the meaningful difference is measured using the effect size criterion rather than the statistical significance criterion. Moreover, larger samples are extremely helpful in estimation studies since they would yield smaller standard errors and smaller confidence interval estimates.

Rather than using extremely large sample sizes, researchers whose main interest is hypothesis testing are encouraged to use efficient sample sizes that have adequate statistical power to detect meaningful differences for a predetermined effect size. A complete elaboration of how this can be accomplished for studies having two independent samples is given in McNamara (1991). A more theoretical treatment of statistical power for a wide variety of common behavioral science statistics tests is given in Cohen (1988).

Note 12 – It is important to recognize that 50 percent of the Method One scores exceed their sample mean of 90. Hence, a larger percent of these Method One scores will automatically exceed a lower score of 78.

Also of interest, one can get the same 38 percent advantage by using the Method One normal distribution which has a mean of 90 and a standard deviation of 10. For this normal distribution, a score of 78 (the Method Two sample mean) has a z score value of negative 1.2 which is the 12th percentile in this distribution. Since a score of 90 is the 50th percentile in the same normal distribution, the advantage percent favoring Method One is again 38 percent.

Note 13 – A closer examination of the last column of Table 2.7 can be very informative. Notice first that an effect size of zero has a zero percent advantage. This corresponds to the case where two equal sample means are encountered.

Also observe that the larger the effect size, the larger the advantage percent. In addition, notice that there is *not* an exact linear relationship between effect size values and advantage percents.

Absence of an exact linear relationship between effect size values and advantage percents can be easily verified. For example, the advantage percent for an effect size of 0.5 is 19 percent. The advantage percent for an effect size of 1.0 is 34 percent and for 1.5 is 43 percent. Clearly, increasing effect sizes by increments of 0.5 does not yield a constant increase in advantage percents. Specifically, moving from 0.5 to 1.0 increases the advantage percent by 15 percent. Moving from 1.0 to 1.5 increases the advantage percent by 9 percent.

Finally, since the relationship between the effect size and the advantage percent is *not* an exact linear relationship, one should never infer that an effect size twice as large as another automatically implies that its advantage percent is also twice as large.

Note 14 – Once a specific effect size criterion of interest is determined, statistical power calculations can be made to determine an efficient sample size. For example, given both alpha and beta set at 0.05, a nondirectional alternative statistical hypothesis, and a desire to detect an effect size of 0.50, the required sample size to ensure statistical power at 0.95 is 105 students in each sample.

If alpha and beta were both set at 0.01 to further minimize possible inferential errors, H(A) remained nondirectional and the effect size criterion was still 0.50, the required sample size to ensure statistical power (1-beta) equal to 0.99 is just 194 students in each sample.

Details on how this straightforward sample size procedure works when the effect size criterion is specified before the equipment is undertaken are given in McNamara (1991).

Note 15—The effect size estimates are excellent predictors of what is likely to happen in the case study district when both methods correspond explicitly to the two methods under investigation by the district. If the two methods are similar rather than identical, the effect size estimates derived using Table 2.8 procedures are still helpful.

In most prior research studies, effect sizes are not entered into the article. This poses no problem to the task force because all that is needed to use the Table 2.8 procedure are the sample sizes, sample means and standard deviations for the two experimental groups. These are the same inputs required to calculate the traditional t test statistic. Thus, they are usually available in the research article.

Assume the comparable district visited in the initial task of the school improvement search did not publish its findings on the new versus old method of teaching Algebra I. A Table 2.8 effect size estimate can still be calculated using the test information (sample sizes, means and standard deviations) available in the district's records.

Those interested in meta-analysis should consider reading Borg (1988, Chapter 5) and Borg and Gall (1989, Chapter 5). Both sources are nontechnical. More theoretical treatments of meta-analysis are given in several sources. Two good starting sources are Shaver (1991) and Hedges and Becker (1986). Both of these sources have excellent reference lists for further reading.

PROBLEMS

Three specific problems are given here for those who wish to verify that they can use the effect size procedures specified in this chapter. All three problems can be done without reference to other research materials. Solutions for these three problems are given in the back of the book.

Problem 2.1

Assume that an innovative school district wishes to repeat the Algebra I experimental study summarized in Table 2.1. A random sample of 400 Algebra I students is selected. These 400 students are randomly assigned to the two teaching methods so that there are 200 students in each of these two experimental samples. The following outcome data are observed:

- $M(1) = 89$ (Mean for Method One Sample)
- $M(2) = 79$ (Mean for Method Two Sample)
- $S(1) = 11$ (Standard deviation for Method One Sample)
- $S(2) = 9$ (Standard deviation for Method Two Sample)

Your first task is to determine the common standard deviation for this fair-test experiment using the procedure detailed in Table 2.4. Your solution to this problem should be a table that is identical in form to the one given in Table 2.5. Remember that a sample variance is the square of the sample standard deviation.

Problem 2.2

Your second task is to calculate and interpret the effect size for this fair-test experiment. Your solution to this problem should be a table that is identical in form to Table 2.6.

Problem 2.3

Your third task is to answer these two questions. First, which method was the more effective strategy for teaching Algebra I? Second, how would you communicate this difference to policy makers and practitioners without reference to technical statistical terms? (Hint: Use your effect size result from Problem 2.2 and the effect size information given in Table 2.7.)

REFERENCES

Babbie, E. 1990. *Survey Research Methods, 2nd Ed.* Belmont: Wadsworth.

Ball, D. L. and T. L. Schroeder. 1992. "Implementing the Professional Standards for Teaching Mathematics," *Mathematics Teacher*, 85(1):67–72.

Borg, W. A. 1988. *Applying Educational Research: A Practical Guide for Teachers, 2nd Ed.* New York: Longman.

Borg, W. A. and M. Gall. 1989. *Educational Research, 5th Ed.* New York: Longman.

Christensen, L. B. 1988. *Experimental Methodology, 4th Ed.* Boston: Allyn and Bacon.

Cohen, J. 1988. *Statistical Power for the Behavioral Sciences, 2nd Ed.* Hillsdale, NJ: Lawrence Erlbaum.

Fraenkel, J. R. and N. E. Wallen. 1990. *How to Design and Evaluate Research in Education*, New York: McGraw-Hill.

Hedges, L. V. and B. J. Becker. 1986. "Statistical Methods in the Meta-Analysis of Research on Gender Differences," in *The Psychology of Gender*, J. Shibley Hyde and M. C. Linn, eds., Baltimore: The Johns Hopkins University Press.

Issac, S. and W. B. Michael. 1981. *Handbook in Research and Evaluation for Education and the Behavioral Sciences, 2nd Ed.* San Diego: EDITS Publishers.

Kysh, J. 1991. "Implementing the Curriculum and Evaluation Standards: First-Year Algebra," *Mathematics Teacher*, 84(12): 715–722.

McNamara, J. F. 1991. "Statistical Power in Educational Research," *National Forum of Applied Educational Research Journal*, 3(2): 23–26.

Mitchell, M. and J. Jolley. 1988. *Research Design Explained.* New York: Holt, Rinehart and Winston.

Popham, J. W. and K. A. Sirotnik. 1992. *Understanding Statistics in Education.* Itasaca, IL: Peacock.

Shavelson, R. J. 1988. *Statistical Reasoning for the Behavioral Sciences, 2nd Ed.* Boston: Allyn and Bacon.

Shaver, J. P. 1991. "Quantitative Reviewing of Research," in *Handbook of Research on Social Studies Teaching and Learning*, J. P. Shaver, ed., New York: Macmillan.

CHAPTER 3

Statistical Power in School Improvement Research

THE National Academy of Education was founded in 1965 to promote scholarly inquiry concerning the ends and means of education. Recognition of the need to better understand the nature of research in education and its potential contribution to school reform led the Academy to appoint the Committee on Educational Research. The Committee's specific commission was to study the issues and publish its conclusions on how the educational community could make more effective use of research and scholarship to improve classroom instruction and the administration of schools.

Research for Tomorrow's Schools was the Committee's published report. Since its release in 1969, this book has been used extensively. In the 1970s its findings and recommendations were frequently referenced to clarify expectations for the emerging field of educational evaluation and policy studies. More recently, it has been reexamined to pinpoint how school/university collaborative research can be used to bridge the gap between theory and practice.

The direction taken in this column has been influenced by a key distinction advanced in this landmark report. Convinced that the popular labels "basic research" and "applied research" fail to capture essential distinctions between the kinds of studies that inform educational practitioners and policy makers, the Academy's Committee on Educational Research proposed the distinction between *decision-oriented* and *conclusion-oriented* research.

In a decision-oriented study, the investigator is asked to provide information wanted by a decision maker. Decision-oriented

53

studies are commissioned studies. Specifically, decision makers first acknowledge the need for information to guide their actions. With these information needs in mind, they pose questions to the investigator.

Investigators in decision-oriented research are not free to chase interesting sidelights, but rather they are expected to deliver answers to practical questions. Moreover, schedules and deadlines for reporting findings are almost always a part of the commission accepted by the investigator.

The conclusion-oriented study, on the other hand, takes its direction from the investigator's interest and informed conjectures. Investigators formulate their own questions, which are usually general ones rather than questions about a specific institution.

The aim of conclusion-oriented inquiry is to conceptualize and understand the phenomena of interest. Since schedules and deadlines are not imposed, investigators are free to add new questions or to take advantage of the early insights to redirect their inquiries.

From this description, it should be clear that conclusion-oriented studies are not planned with an eye to a definite and useful result. Their value can be judged only after the studies are completed and conclusions are shared with the profession (see Note 1).

In framing this distinction, the Committee went to great lengths to declare that neither type of research was preferred over the other. In fact, they noted that the two types of research have distinct functions and, more important, depend upon each other to advance knowledge about education and schooling.

The Commission was also clear in noting that the distinction between decision-oriented and conclusion-oriented research does *not* depend on the research method used in the investigation. Any particular research method can be applied in either type of inquiry. Thus, demographic analysis, ethnographic methods, historical criticism, philosophical interpretation, surveys, computer simulations or experiments can be used in either decision-oriented or conclusion-oriented investigations.

In a word, it is not the research topic or the research method, but the conditions under which the study takes place that is emphasized in the National Academy of Education's distinction between decision-oriented and conclusion-oriented research. The focus of this book has been on decision-oriented research. The first two chapters dealt explicitly with the use of surveys and experiments as research strategies that inform decision makers and decision making in schools.

In the first chapter, surveys were discussed in terms of reviewing a school district's decision regarding year-round school programs. The second chapter focused on the value of a single comparative experiment to help a school district reach a decision about the effectiveness of a new teaching method to increase student achievement (see Note 2).

The intent of this article is to continue to explore exactly what is involved in conducting comparative experiments. While the second article focused on the effect size criterion to define meaningful differences and to evaluate experimental outcomes, this article is used to discuss the importance of statistical power in designing comparative experiments.

Using both the general school improvement research focus and the single school district case study developed for the discussion of the effect size criterion, this article provides responses to three specific questions on statistical power. These are:

1. What is statistical power?
2. Why is statistical power an important consideration in school improvement research projects?
3. How can one maximize the statistical power of a proposed school improvement research project?

With this in mind, the article is divided into three parts, each part providing an answer to one of these questions.

Taken collectively, and in the order specified above, answers to these three questions provide school improvement (decision-oriented) researchers efficient sample sizes to guarantee the statistical validity of their experimental research findings.

WHAT IS STATISTICAL POWER?

In practical terms, *statistical power is the ability to detect a true difference when, in fact, a true difference exists in the population of interest.* Put another way, statistical power is a kind of in-surance policy. It guarantees that the actual study we propose is almost certain to detect a true difference if there really is one in the population of interest.

This detection concern can be easily explained using a specific school improvement research project. Let us again assume (as we did in the second article on the effect size criterion) that a school district's task force has uncovered what they believe is a more ef-fective strategy for teaching Algebra I courses in their district.

Research Design

With this alternative in hand, the second task for this action research group would be to design and conduct a fair-test experi-ment that compares the performance of the district's Algebra I students exposed to the new experimental method with those who are taught Algebra I using the traditional method (the method used in prior years).

An overview of the correct research design for this case study is given in Table 3.1. The experimental results for this fair-test experiment are entered in the top right-hand corner of the table.

This experimental outcome measure reflects a summary of results (means and standard deviations) for the two sample groups on a standardized Algebra I examination known to have excellent content validity in terms of the district's Algebra I cur-riculum guide.

If this school improvement research group used the effect size criterion approach specified in McNamara (1992b), the research design developed in task two would include an operational definition (decision rule) for a meaningful difference.

Effect Size Decision Rule

Let us assume that a *minimum* effect size of 0.50 was specified as the decision rule for defining a meaningful difference. This task two decision rule (specified prior to conducting the fair-test experiment) acknowledges that the case study district would be willing to adopt the new Algebra I teaching method in all senior

Table 3.1. The Algebra I experimental study.

Research Hypothesis: The experimental method (#1) is more effective than the traditional method (#2).

Verification Strategy: Design and conduct a true experiment to verify the claim made in the research hypothesis.

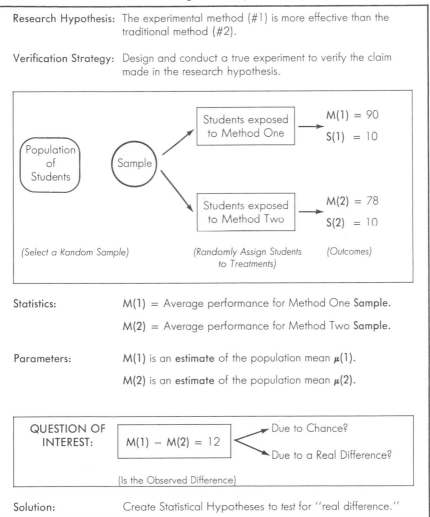

Statistics: M(1) = Average performance for Method One **Sample**.

M(2) = Average performance for Method Two **Sample**.

Parameters: M(1) is an **estimate** of the population mean $\mu(1)$.

M(2) is an **estimate** of the population mean $\mu(2)$.

QUESTION OF INTEREST:	M(1) − M(2) = 12	← Due to Chance?
		← Due to a Real Difference?
	(Is the Observed Difference)	

Solution: Create Statistical Hypotheses to *test* for "real difference."

high schools if the fair-test experiment had an actual effect size equal to or greater than 0.50 favoring Method One (see Note 3).

Practically speaking, declaring an effect size of 0.50 means the district would invest in Method One if it demonstrated that an additional 19 percent (or more) of its Algebra I students had better performance scores when taught by Method One rather than Method Two.

Analysis of Experimental Results

The third task in the school improvement case study is used to reevaluate the task force's belief (research hypothesis) regarding the increased effectiveness of the new alternative teaching strategy (Method One).

In this final task, the actual results of the fair-test experiment from Table 3.1 are expressed as an effect size. This analysis is given in Table 3.2. Given a common standard deviation of 10 and a sample mean difference of 12, the actual effect size for the experiment is 1.2.

Using the effect size criterion approach, the task force would recognize that the actual experimental effect size of 1.2 was larger than the decision rule effect size of 0.50. Accordingly, they would recommend that Method One be adopted in all of the district's senior high schools.

Table 3.2. Calculating and interpreting effect sizes.

Formula
ES = SMD divided by CSD ES = 12 divided by 10 = 1.2
Legend ES = the effect size estimate SMD = the sample mean differences CSD = the common standard deviation
Interpretation Given the Algebra I experiment having a 12 point sample mean difference favoring students taught by method one, and a common standard deviation equal to 10 points, the effect size estimate is 1.2. This effect size estimate has the following interpretation: On average, students taught by Method One have performance scores **that are 1.2 standard deviations higher** than the performance scores for students taught by Method Two.

All that needs to be communicated to anyone interested in the outcome of the experiment is this straightforward statement: An effect size value of 1.2 tells us that an additional 38 percent of the district's Algebra I students had better achievement test scores when taught by the new teaching method rather than the teaching method used in previous school years (see Note 4).

WHY IS STATISTICAL POWER IMPORTANT?

With an overview of this school improvement case study in place, the importance of statistical power can be explained in a concrete way.

Let us assume the case study school district task force was concerned about the statistical power of their fair-test experiment. This group would have asked the following question in the design phase of stage two: If a true difference in student performance favoring Method One (the new alternative teaching method) does exist in our district, what are the chances the experiment we are about to implement will detect this difference in student achievement?

Since statistical power is the actual probability of finding a true population difference when, in fact, a true population difference exists, we can be sure the school district's task force would prefer to be 100 percent certain (a probability equal to 1.0) that the actual experiment they implement will find this meaningful difference.

Effect Size Decision Rule

Thinking in terms of the task force's effect size decision rule which was set at 0.50, detecting a true population difference (if it does exist) would imply that the task force has found a new teaching method that will increase the Algebra I achievement of at least another 19 percent of its students.

To put this advantage into perspective, consider an urban school district having a total of 4,000 students enrolled in Algebra I courses. Uncovering an effect size of 0.50 in their fair-test experiment would mean this school district has found a new teaching method that will increase the Algebra I achievement of an additional 760 students.

This advantage is clearly *not* restricted to the size of a district's student population. It holds for any size. For example, consider a school district having just one high school and 300 students enrolled in Algebra I courses. Finding an effect size of 0.50 favoring Method One in this district would imply that an additional fifty-seven students would have higher Algebra I achievement scores when all students are taught using this new teaching method (see Note 5).

Design Strategy

Given the possibility of finding this very attractive achievement advantage, a task force would not wish to design an experiment having an extremely small probability of detecting this advantage. Yet it is very possible that a small probability of detecting this advantage could result if sample sizes used in the proposed experiment are too small.

Sample Size Alternatives

How the small probability of detecting this advantage could arise can be understood by examining Table 3.3. This table provides a simulation that identifies the statistical power values corresponding to various sample sizes the Algebra I case study task force might have selected for its fair-test experiment. The simulation is based on using the task force's effect size decision rule equal to 0.50.

Entries in Table 3.3 have a straightforward interpretation. Columns one and two of this table are used to let the possible sample sizes vary from a small sample of twenty students in each of the two experimental groups to a very large sample having 500 students in each group.

Column three of Table 3.3 identifies the corresponding statisti-

Table 3.3. Statistical power for selected two-group experiments.

Sample Size per Group	Total Sample Size	Statistical Power	Error Probability
20	40	0.33	0.67
30	60	0.47	0.53
35	70	0.54	0.46
40	80	0.60	0.40
50	100	0.70	0.30
75	150	0.86	0.14
100	200	0.94	0.06
150	300	0.99	0.01
500	1,000	1.00	0.00

Note: Table values are based on those reported in Cohen (1988) for an independent sample t test with alpha predetermined at 0.05, a nondirectional alternative statistical hypothesis, and an effect size of 0.50 used as the decision rule for inferring a meaningful difference between the two populations under study. Row one has the following interpretation. Given a declared effect size of interest to be 0.50 and a total sample size of forty (with two equal group samples of twenty), the statistical power for detecting this effect size is 0.33. The probability of failing to detect this effect size is 0.67. Also notice the general rule: as sample size increases, statistical power increases and the corresponding error probability decreases.

cal power for each sampling design. For example, if just twenty students each were assigned to the Method One and Method Two samples, the probability of detecting a 0.50 effect size difference is just 0.33.

A statistical power value of 0.33 implies that this research design has only a one-third chance of detecting the 0.50 effect size difference.

Column four of Table 3.3 identifies the error probability for the sampling design. For example, if the statistical power is 0.33, the error probability of this sampling design is one minus 0.33 or 0.67. This error probability suggests that a sampling design with twenty students in each group has a 67 percent chance of failing to detect a true difference between the two methods.

Since the ability to detect and report meaningful differences between the two teaching methods is the task force's primary purpose, it is safe to say that this sampling plan is not very efficient for this purpose.

Other entries in Table 3.3 can be interpreted in a similar manner. For example, consider the column one entry for a sampling design with 50 students in each group. The statistical power of this sampling design is increased to 0.70 and the corresponding error probability is reduced to 0.30.

Increasing this sample size by a factor of two yields a sampling design with 100 students in each experimental group. If this design were implemented by the task force, the statistical power would be 0.94 and the corresponding error probability would be just 0.06.

Clearly this sampling design is far superior to the first one where just twenty students were in each group. By using 100 students per group rather than just twenty per group, the ability to detect an effect size of 0.50 has increased from 0.33 to 0.94. Thus, the ability to detect a true population difference of interest to the task force (and the decision makers to whom they must report) has increased dramatically from 33 percent to 94 percent.

In terms of the detection objective reflected in this simulation, Shavelson (1988) suggests "researchers should take a power trip." He believes they should strive to design the most powerful experimental inquiry possible. On this point, he notes "there seems little reason to spend time and money on an experiment which has little chance of detecting a difference when the difference is actually there" (p. 285).

The Bottom Line

What should be clear from examining Table 3.3 is the following: *As sample size increases and an effect size value is held constant, statistical power increases, and the corresponding error probability is reduced.*

With this generalization in mind, we can turn to the third and final question that focuses on how one goes about maximizing the statistical power of a proposed experiment.

Clearly, maximizing statistical power should be the direction taken in the research design planning stage of any decision-oriented research project. Determining statistical power after the fact can sometimes be a disappointing experience, especially when researchers find out that the sampling plan they implemented had only a very small chance of detecting a real difference.

HOW IS STATISTICAL POWER MAXIMIZED?

The strategy for answering the third question begins by offering the conclusion first. This conclusion is then followed by an explanation of the formal theoretical properties from statistical inference needed to justify this result.

The conclusion is as follows: Maximizing statistical power requires a researcher to specify four essential inferential decision rules in the research design planning phase. Once *all* four decision rules are specified, the most efficient (actually the smallest) sample size needed to ensure the desired level of statistical power can be easily identified using a published sample size table.

This conclusion is illustrated in Table 3.4. The four essential decision rules specified in steps one through four and the correct use of the published sample size tables in step five will be explained in the justification offered below.

If the sampling design solution given in Table 3.4 were used in the Algebra I case study, the district's task force would have a 95 percent chance of finding a real difference (a 19 percent advantage) in student performance, if it were present in their school district.

Theoretical justification for this result requires one to walk

Table 3.4. Procedure for determining sample size.

Step One: Specify alpha to minimize the risk of a Type I error.
Decision Rule One: Set alpha at 0.05.

Step Two: Specify beta to minimize the risk of a Type II error.
Decision Rule Two: Set beta at 0.05.

Step Three: Indicate the type of alternative statistical hypothesis.
Decision Rule Three: Declare a nondirectional alternative statistical hypothesis to be used in the hypothesis testing model.

Step Four: Declare the desired effect size criterion.
Decision Rule Four: Set the effect size at 0.50.

Step Five: Select required sample size from sampling table.
Given the four decision rules specified above, the random sampling design used in the experiment would require a total sample size of 210 with two equal samples of 105 each. Since beta is 0.05 in the second decision rule, the statistical power is 0.95.

through the actual logic and procedures used in inferential statistics. This justification, given below, is organized in four parts. The Algebra I case study is used to illustrate key concepts.

Part One: Statistical Inference as Decision Making

In making statistical inferences, Shavelson (1988) suggests that the researcher assumes the role of a decision maker. The decision issue is to reject or fail to reject the null statistical hypothesis indicating no difference.

For the Algebra I case study, the correct null statistical hypothesis is given in step one in Table 3.5. The symbol for this hypothesis is H(0).

To be absolutely certain about reaching a correct decision, a researcher would have to measure every person in the population. In many school improvement research studies, this certainty requirement is impractical.

Accordingly, the researcher usually operates under conditions of uncertainty and draws a random sample from the population of interest (see Table 3.1). Using data from the random sample and a test statistic, the researcher infers what is true of the population. Based on these test results, the researcher decides whether or not to reject the null statistical hypothesis. This procedure is illustrated in Table 3.5.

Decision Problem

Whenever researchers use sample data to estimate a population difference, there is always some degree of uncertainty about whether the difference of the sample means accurately reflects the true population difference. Hence, researchers must make an inference from sample data to decide whether or not a true difference exists.

This decision problem can be seen in Table 3.1. Note that two alternatives exist for the 12 point difference encountered in the Algebra I case study experiment. This difference could be *due to chance* (happened only because of sampling error) or *due to a real difference* (one teaching method is actually more effective).

Table 3.5. Hypotheses and decision rules for the Algebra I experiment.

Step One: Indicate the statistical hypotheses

Null Hypothesis   H(0): $\mu(1)$ equals $\mu(2)$
Alternative Hypothesis   H(A): $\mu(1)$ is *not* equal to $\mu(2)$

H(0) is a statistical null hypothesis indicating that the two methods of teaching Algebra I are equally effective.

H(A) is a statistical alternative hypothesis indicating that the two methods of teaching Algebra I are *not* equally effective.

$\mu(1)$ is a parameter indicating the mean performance score for the district's Algebra I student population when all students are taught using Method One.

$\mu(2)$ is a parameter indicating the mean performance score for the district's Algebra I student population when all students are taught using Method Two.

Step Two: Specify the decision rules for evaluating H(0)

Reject H(0) if the effect size value observed exceeds 0.50

Retain H(0) if the effect size value observed does *not* exceed 0.50

Step Three: Calculate the test statistic for the experiment

The essential input information needed to calculate the observed effect size for the two independent samples is as follows:

- Sample mean for Method One is **90.**
- Sample mean for Method Two is **78.**
- Sample mean difference is **12.**
- Common standard deviation is **10.**

Inserting this information into the effect size formula, the observed test statistic value for this experiment is 1.2.

Step Four: Indicate the decision regarding H(0)

The observed effect size value of 1.2 exceeds the decision rule effect size value of 0.50 specified in step two above. Thus, H(0) is rejected and a meaningful significant difference favoring Method One is detected.

Step Five: Interpret the statistical test findings

Given a meaningful significant difference favoring Method One, the researcher would conclude that Method One was a more effective method for teaching Algebra I in the district where the experiment was conducted.

Statistical Hypotheses

This decision problem has two features. First, there is the true situation in the population. Second, there is a need to infer the true situation from the sample data. This decision problem can be put into the familiar hypothesis testing model for comparing the results from two independent samples (see Note 6).

This has been done for the Algebra I case study in Table 3.5. In step one the researcher formulates two statistical hypotheses. $H(0)$ in Table 3.5 equates $\mu(1)$ to $\mu(2)$.

This null hypothesis suggests that the two parameters (population values) are equal, implying that any observed difference in the two samples is due only to chance. Thus, $H(0)$ for this experiment places the two parameters in an equation to infer that the two Algebra I teaching methods are equally effective.

Since $H(0)$ might not be true, the researcher needs to specify an alternative statistical hypothesis. Accordingly, step one in Table 3.5 specifies $H(A)$, an alternative statistical hypothesis that fits this logical requirement. Note, $H(0)$ and $H(A)$ are complementary. This implies that they have no overlap and that between them they exhaust all possible outcomes of the experiment.

Correct Decisions

In the population, $H(0)$ is either true or false. When the sample data are linked with the decision rule (see step two in Table 3.5), the researcher may decide to reject or not reject $H(0)$. This decision could be correct or incorrect. This decision situation is depicted in Table 3.6.

A careful examination of Table 3.6 indicates researchers can make correct decisions when they decide (a) *not* to reject a true null hypothesis or (b) to reject a false null hypothesis. These two correct decision possibilities are labeled Case 1 and Case 4.

Incorrect Decisions

Table 3.6 also indicates that researchers can make two types of errors. A Type I Error occurs when researchers incorrectly reject a true null hypothesis. This possibility is given in Case 3.

Table 3.6. The decision problem in hypothesis testing.

		H(0) IS TRUE	H(0) IS FALSE
	DO NOT REJECT H(0)	Correct Decision Case 1	Incorrect Decision Type II Error Case 2
Decision alternatives based on inferences from sample data	REJECT H(0)	Incorrect Decision Type I Error Case 3	Correct Decision Case 4

Interpretation:

Statistical Hypothesis. H(0) is the null statistical hypothesis. For two independent samples, H(0) declares that the true population means (parameters) for the two groups under investigation are equal. Hence, H(0) implies that there is no difference in the two groups.

Logical Errors. Since the true population is not known, researchers use data from random samples and a statistical test to infer what is true in the population of interest. This inferential decision-making process must guard against two possible errors. These are Type I errors (see Case 3) and Type II errors (see Case 2).

Actual Error. Once a specific statistical test of H(0) is conducted, only one correct or incorrect decision is possible. Thus, only one actual error occurs each time an inferential decision is made. Specifically,

When the researcher's inferential decision results in not rejecting H(0), there are only two possibilities.

If H(0) is true in the population, a **correct** decision was made (see Case 1).

If H(0) is false in the population, an **incorrect** decision was made, resulting in a Type II Error (see Case 2).

When the researcher's inferential decision results in rejecting H(0), there are only two possibilities.

If H(0) is true in the population, an **incorrect** decision was made, resulting in a Type I Error (see Case 3).

If H(0) is false in the population, a **correct** decision was made (see Case 4).

Decision Strategy. Since the true situation in the population of interest is not known, researchers should use random samples and statistical tests that minimize the probability of committing either type of inferential error.

Researchers can make another type of error in situations where the null hypothesis is false. Specifically, a Type II Error occurs when researchers incorrectly fail to reject (do *not* reject) a false null hypothesis. This possibility is given in Case 2 in Table 3.6.

Logical Versus Actual Errors

While the decision problem charted in Table 3.6 specifies two logical errors, only one of these two types of errors can occur in testing a specific null hypothesis.

This can be illustrated using Table 3.6. If the application of the effect size decision rule (specified in step two in Table 3.5) leads the researcher to reject $H(0)$, only the bottom row of Table 3.6 needs to be examined. If $H(0)$ is true in the population, an incorrect decision was made (see Case 3). If $H(0)$ is false in the population, a correct decision was made (see Case 4).

On the other hand, if the effect size decision rule leads the researcher *not* to reject (retain) $H(0)$, then only the top row of Table 3.6 would be examined. Once again, there would be only one correct decision (see Case 1) and one incorrect decision (see Case 2).

Part Two: Error Probabilities

Since statistical decision makers must operate under conditions of uncertainty, applications of statistical inference must be concerned with both types of errors. This concern can be expressed in terms of error probabilities that accurately reflect the risk of committing either a Type I or Type II error.

Alpha

To avoid a Type I error, researchers frequently set the level of statistical significance at 0.05. In inferential terms, the level of significance is called alpha.

The precise inferential specification is as follows: The probability of committing a Type I error is alpha. This specification emphasizes the distinction between a Type I error as a logical consideration and alpha as a probability specified in the inferential model to cover this logical possibility.

Beta

To avoid a Type II error, researchers should (but seldom do) specify a predetermined probability to cover this potential error. In inferential terms, this probability is called beta.

Similarly, the precise inferential specification is stated as follows: The probability of committing a Type II error is called beta. Once again, this expression helps to distinguish between a Type II error as a logical possibility and beta as a predetermined probability to cover this inferential error.

Four Essential Probabilities

It must be kept in mind that the true situation in the population is not known by the researcher. Accordingly, four probabilities are operating each time one tests a hypothesis about a difference in the population using sample data and a test statistic. Two of these probabilities are alpha and beta. The other two probabilities are associated with making a correct decision and can be expressed as complements to alpha and beta.

The probability of correctly retaining H(0) when it is true in the population is one minus alpha. The probability of correctly rejecting H(0) is one minus beta. The formal name of this probability is statistical power.

All four of these probabilities and their influence on the decision about retaining or rejecting H(0) are summarized in the top half of Table 3.7.

Part Three: Sampling Designs

The best strategy for guarding against either type of error in a proposed sampling design is to specify *low* probabilities for both alpha and beta. Moreover, if a researcher believes it is equally

Table 3.7. Four probabilities specified in hypothesis testing.

Since the true situation in the population is not known by the researcher, four probabilities are operating each time a researcher tests a hypothesis about a true difference in the population using sample data and a test statistic. These are:

Probability of incorrectly rejecting a true H(0) = Alpha.
Probability of correctly retaining a true H(0) = 1 − Alpha.
Probability of incorrectly retaining a false H(0) = Beta.
Probability of correctly rejecting a false H(0) = 1 − Beta.

H(0) is a statistical null hypothesis specifying no difference in the population. Its truth is unknown to the researcher.

In practice, a researcher specifies the two error probabilities which are alpha and beta. In the Algebra I case study example, both alpha and beta were set at 0.05. Accordingly, the four exact probabilities for testing the hypothesis about a difference between the two teaching methods were:

Probability of incorrectly rejecting a true H(0) = 0.05.
Probability of correctly retaining a true H(0) = (1 − 0.05) = 0.95.
Probability of incorrectly retaining a false H(0) = 0.05.
Probability of correctly rejecting a false H(0) = (1 − 0.05) = 0.95.

The statistical null hypothesis in this case study indicates that there is no difference in the effectiveness of the two teaching methods. Its truth is unknown to the researcher.

---

important to guard against Type I and Type II errors, equal *low* probabilities should be specified for both alpha and beta (see Note 7).

This strategy was used in the five-step sampling design solution provided in Table 3.4. Each step of this solution strategy is reviewed below.

In step one, alpha was set at 0.05. This error probability acknowledges that the risk of a Type I error is five percent.

In step two, beta was also set at 0.05. This error probability acknowledges that the risk of a Type II error is also five percent.

Since alpha and beta were both set at 0.05, the researcher is clearly indicating that it is equally important to guard against both types of errors.

All four of the probabilities resulting from the specifications given in these first two steps are entered in the bottom half of Table 3.7. Note that setting beta at 0.05 also indicates that the desired statistical power for the proposed sampling design is equal to 0.95.

In step three, a nondirectional alternative statistical hypothesis was specified. This hypothesis allows $H(0)$ to be rejected if a real difference favoring either group is detected (see Note 8).

Next, step four in the Table 3.4 solution was used to specify a desired effect size equal to 0.50 (see Note 9).

Finally, step five was used to determine the minimum sample size needed to ensure a statistical power equal to 0.95. This minimum sample size was located in a published sample size table using all four essential decision rules given in the four previous steps. *If any one of the four essential decision rules is not specified, the published sample size tables can not be used.*

Sample size tables for a statistical test involving two independent samples (the research design used in the Algebra I case study) are now available in many behavioral science statistics texts (see Note 10). For the four decision rules given in Table 3.4, these tables indicate a total required sample size of 210 students (with 105 students placed in each group) is needed to ensure a statistical power equal to 0.95.

Sampling Design Options

Required sample sizes for three of the most common sampling design options used in educational research are presented in Table 3.8. Given the theoretical framework developed above, the logic behind these three sampling design options is now easy to grasp.

First, recall from Table 3.4 that four essential decision rules

Table 3.8. Sample sizes for three basic research designs.

Design Options	Effect Size	Alpha Value	Beta Value	Sample Size per Group
Design One	0.50	0.01	0.01	194
Design Two	0.50	0.05	0.05	105
Design Three	0.50	0.10	0.10	69

Note: Sample size requirements are based on those reported in Cohen (1988) for an independent sample t test where the researcher wishes to detect an effect size of 0.50 using a nondirectional alternative statistical hypothesis. Design Two can be interpreted as follows. The level of significance desired is alpha which equals 0.05. Statistical power is one minus beta which equals 0.95. Thus, to achieve a statistical power of 0.95, Design Two would require a total sample size of 210 with two equal samples of 105 per group.

must be specified to ensure that a desired statistical power is present in an actual sampling design one wishes to implement.

Next, it is important to notice that Table 3.8 assumes that the researcher wishes to change *only* the error probabilities associated with decision rule one (alpha) and decision rule two (beta).

Finally, note that both decision rule three (the use of a non-directional alternative hypothesis) and decision rule four (a desired effect size equal to 0.50) are not altered. That is, they are the same for all three designs. With this information in hand, all three Table 3.8 design options have a straightforward explanation.

First Option

Informed researchers often begin their search for a required sample size by indicating that they want the risk for Type I and Type II errors to have the same probability. If they also want to use the convention of setting the significance level (alpha) at 0.05, then design two in Table 3.8 would be their choice.

This design was also given in Table 3.4. It requires the researcher to use a random sample of 105 students per group. The statistical power of this design is 0.95. Thus, a researcher who implements this design has a 95 percent chance of finding a true effect size difference of 0.50 in the population of interest (see Note 11).

Second Option

If the design two option is not feasible in the research setting of interest, researchers might consider implementing design three. In this situation, the required sample sizes are reduced to sixty-nine per group. However, the two error probabilities are now both equal to 0.10 and the statistical power is reduced from 0.95 to 0.90 (see Note 12).

Third Option

If researchers have sufficient resources to implement a larger sampling plan, design two might be replaced by design one where both error probabilities are set at 0.01. Note that these error probabilities are very minimal.

If design one were selected, the two sample sizes would increase from 105 to 194, an increase that is still quite feasible in many school districts. This is an excellent sampling decision option. It provides a statistical power of 0.99, which implies that design one would have a 99 percent chance of detecting a true effect size difference of 0.50 in the population of interest.

Best Option

Decreasing alpha and beta to values below 0.01 yields little additional advantage in statistical power. Also, using a nondirectional rather than a directional H(A) makes it more difficult to detect a true difference.

These two facts are frequently used in practical sampling situations. Specifically, setting alpha and beta at 0.01 and using a nondirectional alternative statistical hypothesis is a very efficient way to maximize statistical power for a specific effect size.

With this practical sampling information in hand, the following conclusion holds: The statistical power for detecting a population effect size difference of 0.50 between two groups is maximized when a nondirectional H(A) is declared and the sample size for each group is 194.

This theoretical conclusion has direct application for the Algebra I case study. Specifically, using the nondirectional H(A) and a total sample size of 388 students (with 194 in the Method One sample and 194 in the Method Two sample) will maximize power.

If the district's task force implements this sampling design, it will have a 99 percent chance of detecting an effect size difference of 0.50.

Part Four: Effect Size Alternatives

While an effect size of 0.50 is considered to be a conventional measure of practical significance, school improvement research groups are free to use any effect size decision rule they consider meaningful in their specific situation.

On this point, the National Institute of Education's Joint Dissemination Review Panel observed that an effect size of 0.33 or even one as small as 0.25 is often considered to be educationally significant (see Note 13). Similarly, Borg (1988) suggests that teachers conducting action research projects should feel free to use an effect size of 0.33 to define a meaningful difference.

An array of effect size alternatives that can be used in a school improvement research project is given in Table 3.9.

Thinking in terms of the Algebra I case study, entries in this table can be interpreted as follows. An effect size of 0.33 means the district would invest in Method One (the new teaching alternative) if their experiment demonstrated that an additional 14 percent (or more) of its Algebra I students had better achievement scores when taught by Method One rather than Method Two.

Other entries in Table 3.9 can be interpreted in the same manner by replacing the 14 percent above with the percent given for the effect size of interest. For example, an effect size of 0.25 would use 10 percent, an effect size of 0.40 would use 16 percent, etc.

Table 3.9. Effect size alternatives.

Effect Size	Actual Percents (%)	Adjusted Percents (%)
0.20	7.93	8
0.25	9.87	10
0.30	11.79	12
0.33	13.68	14
0.40	15.50	16
0.50	**19.15**	**19**
0.65	24.22	24
0.80	28.81	29
1.00	34.13	34
1.50	43.32	43
2.00	47.72	48

Note: An effect size of 0.50 is often considered to be a conventional measure of practical significance. Effect size interpretations are usually based on the adjusted percents which are the actual percents rounded to the nearest integer. An effect size of 0.50 has an adjusted percent equal to 19. Thinking in terms of the Algebra I case study used in this article, an effect size of 0.50 would mean that an additional 19 percent of the students had higher achievement scores when taught by Method One rather than Method Two. In general terms, when an effect size of 0.50 is encountered for a research design using a t test for two independent samples, the 19 percent advantage on the criterion of interest (dependent variable) favors the group having the higher sample mean.

Sampling Design Implications

Using effect sizes other than the conventional 0.50 poses no problem since the five-step procedure given in Table 3.4 can be used for any effect size of interest. However, it is important to recognize that the required sample size to maximize statistical power will automatically change as the effect size of interest increases or decreases.

These changes are demonstrated in Table 3.10. This table was constructed for three specific effect sizes. It follows the model used in Table 3.8.

The first segment in Table 3.10 is identical to Table 3.8. The effect size of interest was 0.50. All three sampling designs were discussed in Part Three above. In this discussion, design one was defined as the best sampling design to maximize statistical power for a predetermined effect size of 0.50.

In the second segment, the effect size is *decreased* from 0.50 to 0.30. Next, the strategy used to produce the three designs in Table 3.8 is repeated. Thus, design four is identical to design one with the one exception being that the effect size decision rule is 0.30 rather than 0.50.

Keeping this exception in mind, design five corresponds to design two and design six corresponds to design three. Design four is the best choice design to maximize statistical power.

These correspondences can be verified by comparing the alpha and beta values in Table 3.10. For example, alpha and beta are identical for design one and design four, and so forth.

The last column in the second segment of Table 3.10 gives the three new sample size requirements for adopting an effect size of 0.30. These new values range from 191 in design six to 536 in design four.

In the third segment, this process is repeated by *increasing* the effect size from 0.50 to 0.80. Once again the three-part correspondence can be established. Designs seven, eight and nine correspond to designs one, two and three, respectively. Again, design seven is the best choice design.

These three new sample size requirements are given in the last column of segment three. They range from twenty-seven in

Table 3.10. Sample sizes for nine research designs.

Design Options	Effect Size	Alpha Value	Beta Value	Sample Size per Group
Design One	0.50	0.01	0.01	194
Design Two	0.50	0.05	0.05	105
Design Three	0.50	0.10	0.10	69
Design Four	0.30	0.01	0.01	536
Design Five	0.30	0.05	0.05	290
Design Six	0.30	0.10	0.10	191
Design Seven	0.80	0.01	0.01	77
Design Eight	0.80	0.05	0.05	42
Design Nine	0.80	0.10	0.10	27

Note: Sample size requirements are based on those reported in Cohen (1988) for an independent sample t test where the researcher wishes to detect a particular effect size using a nondirectional alternative statistical hypothesis. Design One can be interpreted as follows. The effect size to be detected is 0.50. The level of significance desired is alpha equal to 0.01. Statistical power is one minus beta which equals to 0.99. Thus, to achieve a statistical power of 0.99, Design One would require a total sample size of 388 with two equal samples of 194 per group.

design nine where statistical power is 0.90 to seventy-seven in design seven where the statistical power is 0.99.

Effect Size and Statistical Power

Analysis of Table 3.10 should yield the following general rule: *As the effect size of interest increases, and the other three decision rules are held constant, the required sample size to maximize statistical power will decrease.*

This general rule can be quickly verified by inspecting the required sample sizes in Table 3.10. For an effect size of 0.30, the required sample size to maximize statistical power is 536 students per group (see design four).

If the effect size of interest is increased to 0.50, the required sample size to maximize statistical power is decreased to 194 students per group (see design one).

Finally, if the effect size is increased again to yield a decision value of 0.80, the required sample size to maximize statistical power is decreased to seventy-seven students per group (see design seven).

This examination of Table 3.10 clearly confirms the general rule above. Specifically, increasing the effect size of interest from 0.30 to 0.50 decreased the required sample size per group from 536 to 194. Increasing the effect size further from 0.50 to 0.80 decreased the sample size from 194 to seventy-seven.

These facts lead to a second generalization that is consistent with the general rule above. It is as follows: *larger effect size differences are far easier to detect than smaller ones.*

This generalization is a very practical insight as well, and one that should be considered in planning school improvement research projects (see Note 14).

SUMMARY

In *Research for Tomorrow's Schools,* the National Academy of Education's Committee on Educational Research proposed the distinction between decision-oriented and conclusion-oriented research. In framing this distinction, the Committee went to great lengths to declare that neither type of research was preferred over the other. In fact, they noted that both types of research have distinct functions. Both provide useful information to improve classroom instruction and the administration of schools. Most important, the Committee believes that the two types of research depend upon each other to advance knowledge about education and schooling.

The Academy's Commission on Educational Research was also clear in noting that the distinction between decision-oriented and conclusion-oriented research does *not* depend on the research strategy used in the investigation. However, the Committee's recommendations clearly emphasized that shortcuts and failures to meet the scientific standards for applying a particular research strategy in either a decision-oriented or conclusion-oriented study are unwarranted and do little to help practitioners and policy makers who seek to build new educational programs on a sound research base.

Influenced directly by the insights in this National Academy of Education report, this article focused on decision-oriented research. Its specific intent was to illustrate why statistical power and effect size decision rules are standard scientific procedures needed to get valid and reliable results in a school improvement research experiment.

Using a single school improvement research case study, it was shown that planning valid scientific experiments in decision-oriented research must begin with the specification of an effect size decision rule. This specification is an important consideration for three reasons.

First, the specification of an effect size decision rule is an information item a researcher must have to conduct a statistical power analysis. Without a specific effect size decision rule, it is impossible to select a statistical power value and to determine the corresponding minimum sample sizes needed to ensure that meaningful differences can be detected.

Second, specification of an effect size decision rule prior to conducting a fair-test experiment is a good administrative practice. It provides school district trustees and practitioners with a specific policy statement to interpret the findings of their experiment.

Third, specification of an effect size decision rule provides a straightforward way to distinguish between statistically significant differences that are trivial and statistically significant differences that are meaningful.

Once an effect size decision rule is in place, research design planning can focus on statistical power which is the ability to detect a true population difference when, in fact, a true population difference exists.

A straightforward five-step method was introduced to determine the statistical power for any experiment a researcher or a school district research group wishes to conduct in order to compare the effectiveness of two alternative methods (see Table 3.4).

The bottom line for this article is given in the following message. The best time for a school improvement research group to specify and decide on the actual statistical power for their investigation is in the research design planning stage. Determining statistical power after the fact can sometimes be a disappointing experience, especially when a school improvement research group finds out that the sampling plan they implemented had no more than a very small chance of detecting a true population difference.

NOTES

Note 1–Throughout the text references to notes are inserted. The text can be read without reference to these notes. Their purpose is threefold: to extend the information provided on theoretical concepts, to identify a few noteworthy sources on the logic of hypothesis testing, and to specify a few guidelines for readers who may wish to conduct a school improvement research experiment using statistical power methods.

The formal reference to *Research for Tomorrow's Schools* is Cronbach and Suppes (1969). The second and third chapters of this book provide an excellent brief history of the evolution of educational research in the United States between 1855 and 1958. Several examples are used to demonstrate how changes in educational thinking have resulted from specific landmark inquiries. Also, the last half of the book provides extensive descriptions and illustrations of conclusion-oriented and decision-oriented research studies.

Note 2–The two articles are cited in the references as McNamara (1992a) on surveys and McNamara (1992b) on comparative experiments. While this article can best be understood as a companion to the second article on comparative experiments in school improvement research, it can be read on its own.

However, it would be useful to know that school improvement research projects, such as the Algebra I case study experiment used here and in McNamara (1992b), typically require a reform group to complete three general tasks. These are: (1) locating an alternative strategy that is likely to be more effective than the current practice, (2) conducting a fair-test experiment that compares the effectiveness of both strategies, and (3) using these comparative test results to reevaluate the belief (research hypothesis) regarding the increased effectiveness of the new alternative strategy.

Note 3 – Wolf (1986) has suggested that an effect size of 0.50 is considered to be a conventional measure of practical significance. Most educational researchers (see Borg, 1988 and Borg and Gall, 1989) agree for two reasons.

First, an effect size of 0.50 will almost always yield a statistically significant difference using a traditional two-tailed t test where the predetermined significance level (alpha) is set at the conventional level of 0.05 and the sample size of each group is at least thirty-five.

Second, uncovering an effect size of 0.50 implies a 19 percent advantage (on the criterion variable of interest) favoring the group having the larger sample mean. A 19 percent advantage is an improvement that is considered to be an extremely meaningful finding in most behavioral science intervention efforts.

It is important to note that selecting a preexperimental effect size is not based on a hard-and-fast rule. For example, Borg (1988) suggests that an effect size of 0.33 is a good indicator of practical significance in action research projects undertaken by classroom teachers. This effect size implies that a sample mean difference between two groups is one-third of a common standard deviation. The corresponding advantage in this case is 14 percent favoring the group with the higher sample mean.

Note 4 – This 38 percent advantage has a straightforward explanation. The Method Two normal curve has a mean of 78 and a standard deviation of 10. For this normal distribution, a score of 90 (the Method One sample mean) has a z score value of 1.2 which is the 88th percentile. Since a score of 78 (the Method Two sample mean) is the 50th percentile in the same normal distribution, the advantage percent favoring Method One is 38 percent.

Note 5 – Practically speaking, whenever an effect size of 0.50 is encountered, it implies that an additional one out of five students in the population under study will score higher on the criterion measure of interest.

Note 6 – Table 3.5 uses the effect size criterion as the test statistic. This test statistic is introduced in step two. If one wishes to use the traditional t test for two independent samples, the same five steps are used in the hypothesis testing model and the critical t test statistic is introduced as the decision rule in step two. This is illustrated in McNamara (1992b).

Guidelines for the use of the hypothesis testing model are given in most basic statistics texts. Two excellent sources on hypothesis testing using the traditional t test for two independent samples are Shavelson (1988, Chapter 13) and Popham and Sirotnik (1992, Chapters 9 and 10).

Note 7—In some proposed investigations, a researcher may believe it is more important to guard against Type I errors than Type II errors. An analogy that illustrates this predisposition is the case where a decision maker believes that it is a much more serious error to convict an innocent person (Type I error) than to fail to convict a guilty person (Type II error).

In an actual hypothesis testing model where it is more important to guard against a Type I error, steps one and two in the Table 3.4 illustration can be modified as follows.

The equal probability values specified for alpha and beta in steps one and two in Table 3.4 would be replaced with unequal probability values that reflect the relative importance of these two error risks.

For example, these values might be alpha equal to 0.05 and beta equal to 0.20. This is a common specification in which a researcher indicates that the risk of a Type I error is four times as important as the risk of a Type II error. This behavioral science convention is discussed in Cohen (1988, p. 56) and in Shavelson (1988, p. 303).

In other investigations, statistical power could be the most important consideration. This situation can arise when the primary intent of a research study is to detect a true positive difference that would favor a highly promising experimental teaching method over an already effective traditional teaching method.

In this situation, the equal probability values specified for alpha and beta in steps one and two of Table 3.4 would be replaced with unequal probability values that reflect the relative importance of these two errors. Given the interest in statistical power, beta would obviously be the smaller probability.

Specifying unequal probabilities for alpha and beta in steps one and two poses no problem for using the basic five-step solution strategy outlined in Table 3.4, because standard sample size tables are constructed to handle either equal or unequal probabilities. However, it is important to keep in mind that the best strategy is to specify low error probabilities for both alpha and beta whenever possible.

Note 8 – A directional alternative statistical hypothesis that is consistent with the research hypothesis in the Algebra I case study would be $\mu(1)$ is greater than $\mu(2)$. In this case, a statistically significant difference is achieved only when the sample mean difference favors Method One.

Specification of a directional or nondirectional H(A) is required when the traditional t test model is used to test H(0). Specifically, a nondirectional H(A) requires a two-tailed t test to detect statistical significance. A directional H(A) requires a one-tailed t test.

Straightforward descriptions of these two testing alternatives in inferential statistics are given in most basic statistics texts such as Shavelson (1988) and Popham and Sirotnik (1992).

In practice, a nondirectional H(A) and a two-tailed t test are usually specified. There are two reasons for this convention.

First, a two-tailed test is a more conservative test. This means it is more difficult to detect statistical significance using a two-tailed rather than a one-tailed test. Put another way, if a two-tailed test yields a statistically significant difference, a one-tailed test for the same sample data will always yield a statistically significant difference. However, the reverse is not always true. That is, statistical significance for a one-tailed test does not automatically imply statistical significance for a two-tailed test.

Second, many researchers such as Shavelson (1988) believe a one-tailed statistical test should be applied only when (a) a theory requires a one-tailed test or (b) there is strong empirical evidence (i.e., several prior research studies) suggesting a consistent direction for the difference between two groups.

Note 9 – In a word, it is impossible to determine the statistical power of a test without specifying an effect size. In addition, there are several reasons why effect sizes should be specified before a study is conducted. These reasons are elaborated in McNamara (1992b).

For the record, the statistical power of any published research article using t tests can be determined even though the researcher did not explicitly address the effect size and statistical power issues in the study. A procedure for how this is done is given in McNamara (1991).

Note 10 – All statistical power values used in this article were located in Cohen (1988, Table 2.4, page 54). This source provides statistical power estimates for all of the most common statistical methods used in behavioral science research.

Abbreviated sample size tables for t test designs having two independent groups can be found in several basic behavioral science statistics texts such as Kirk (1984, p. 475), Shavelson (1988, p. 693) and Hinkle, Wiersma and Jurs (1988, p. 666).

Note 11 – While equal-sized samples are always desirable, it is sometimes impossible in the real world to construct a sampling design having identical sample sizes in each group. In this case, a statistical power of 0.95 can still be achieved for the four essential decision rules of design two.

A brief explanation for how this is done is given below. More specific guidelines are given in Cohen (1988, p. 59).

The need for unequal sample sizes in two-group experiments can arise when a specific experimental method is limited to some fixed number of students or when only a certain number of students can be withheld for use as a control group. Clearly, these situations are likely to occur in some school improvement research projects.

Thinking in terms of the Algebra I case study, let us assume that only seventy-five students can be assigned to Method One, but assigning more students to Method Two is no problem. Also assume that design two is the preferred sampling design. To achieve the desired statistical power of 0.95, the Method Two sample size is determined using the following four-step procedure.

First, get the product of $N(F)$ and N where $N(F)$ is the fixed sample size and N is the required sample size from the sample size tables for the design of interest. Let A be this result. In the case study situation above, $N(F)$ is 75 and N is 105. A is 75 multiplied by 105 which equals 7,875.

Second, let B equal twice the value of $N(F)$. In this example, twice $N(F)$ is twice 75 which equals 150.

Third, let **C** equal **B** minus **N**. In this example **C** equals 150 minus 105 or 45.

Fourth, let **N(V)** be the other required sample size. **N(V)** is equal to **A** from step one divided by **C** from step three. In this example, **N(V)** is 7,875 divided by 45 which equals 175.

Thus, having a Method One sample size of seventy-five and a Method Two sample size of 175 will achieve the same statistical power as a sampling plan having 105 students in each group.

Notice that the example alternative with unequal-sized samples has a larger total required sample size. Specifically, the total sample size required for the example is 175 plus seventy-five which equals 250 students versus two equal sample sizes of 105 which yield a total sample size requirement of 210 students. Thus, the unequal-sized alternative required an additional forty students.

Thinking in terms of Table 3.1, this alternative sampling design could be executed as follows. First, randomly select 250 students to participate in the experiment. Next, randomly select seventy-five students from this sample of 250. Assign these seventy-five students to the Method One sample. The balance of the 250 students, which is 175, would be assigned to the Method Two sample. Everything else done in the experiment would remain unchanged.

The time taken in this note to elaborate the alternative design is time well spent. This is true because the four-step procedure elaborated above can be used for any design to get the two required sample sizes whenever an equal-sized sampling plan cannot be implemented, but **N(F)** is more than **N** divided by two. For example, in the design two situation where **N** was 105, **N(F)**, the fixed sample size, would need to be at least fifty-three.

Since practice makes perfect, it may pay a dividend if the reader applies this procedure one more time. Assume the design of interest is design seven and only fifty students can be assigned to the Method One sample. How many students are required for the Method Two sample? While the details are left to the reader, the answer is 167.

Note 12 – Design three is often implemented when the cost per person in an experiment is very large and only limited funds are available for the experiment. Keep in mind that the efficiency of this design is still very good, especially when compared to a small sampling design where just thirty students are used in each group.

Note 13 – This position is discussed in Tallmadge (1977). Other sources on this point were discussed in Note 3. A more theoretical discussion of effect size options is given in Cohen (1988, Chapter 2). Cohen's "rough" guidelines for effect size decision making suggest that a small effect size is 0.20, a medium effect size is 0.50, and a large effect size is 0.80. However, he is quick to point out that no hard-and-fast rules govern these specifications.

Note 14 – Throughout this article the focus has been on the correct use of experimental methods in the design, implementation and evaluation of school improvement research projects. More to the point, the discussion has focused exclusively on true experiments involving just two independent groups.

The traditional test statistic for evaluating the results of this two-group experiment is the t test for two independent samples.

On the other hand, contemporary statistical methods suggest that effect sizes also be used to evaluate the results of these experiments. Using effect size indicators, researchers can easily recognize the difference between statistically significant findings that are trivial and those that are meaningful. Moreover, effect sizes are required to determine statistical power.

While it was not the intent of this article to discuss the t test for two independent samples in general, all of the statistical methods given here apply to any situation where a traditional t test is used to analyze the information provided in the sample data from two independent groups. On this point, three specific recommendations are advanced.

First, anytime a researcher encounters a traditional t test result that declares a statistically significant difference and ends the analysis at that point, this finding can be (and should be) reevaluated using an effect size measure. This reevaluation can be undertaken using the effect size calculation procedure given in Table 3.2 and the effect size interpretation guidelines given as advantage percents in Table 3.9.

Second, the five-step procedure for determining statistical power given in Table 3.4 can be used before the fact to get the required sample size for any t test situation involving two independent groups. Specifically, the use of this procedure is not restricted to just the experimental investigation discussed here. The procedure can be used to determine the required sample size for any experimental or nonexperimental study involving two independent groups of interest.

Third, the method used to solve the unequal-sized sampling design problem referenced in Note 11 can be applied in any case where the t test for two independent groups is used. Recognizing this fact may help to overcome the mistaken notion that statistical power formulas and tables apply only to the case where equal-sized samples can be entered into a research design.

REFERENCES

Borg, W. A. 1988. *Applying Educational Research: A Practical Guide for Teachers, 2nd Ed.* New York: Longman.

Borg, W. A. and M. Gall. 1989. *Educational Research, 5th Ed.* New York: Longman.

Cohen, J. 1988. *Statistical Power for the Behavioral Sciences, 2nd Ed.* Hillsdale, NJ: Lawrence Erlbaum.

Cronbach, L. J. and P. Suppes, eds. 1969. *Research for Tomorrow's Schools: Disciplined Inquiry for Education.* New York: Macmillan.

Hinkle, D. E., W. Wiersma and S. G. Jurs. 1988. *Applied Statistics for Behavioral Sciences, 2nd Ed.* Boston: Houghton Mifflin.

Kirk, R. E. 1984. *Elementary Statistics, 2nd Ed.* Englewood Cliffs: Prentice-Hall.

McNamara, J. F. 1992. (a) "Sample Sizes for School Preference Surveys," *International Journal of Educational Reform*, 1(1):83–90; (b) "The Effect Size Criterion in School Improvement Research," *International Journal of Educational Reform*, 1(2):191–202.

McNamara, J. F. 1991. "Statistical Power in Educational Research," *National Forum of Applied Educational Research Journal*, 3(2): 23–26.

Popham, J. W. and K. A. Sirotnik. 1992. *Understanding Statistics in Education.* Itasaca, IL: Peacock.

Shavelson, R. J. 1988. *Statistical Reasoning for the Behavioral Sciences, 2nd Ed.* Boston: Allyn and Bacon.

Tallmadge, G. K. 1977. *The Joint Dissemination Review Panel Ideabook.* Washington, DC: National Institute of Education.

Wolf, F. M. 1986. *Meta-Analysis: Quantitative Methods for Research Synthesis.* Beverly Hills: Sage Publications.

CHAPTER 4

Research Designs and Sample Size Requirements in School Improvement Research

ONE of the most difficult problems in designing an educational research project is the sample size issue. This issue is frequently encountered in qualitative as well as quantitative studies. It is encountered in the design of either surveys or experiments. It must also be addressed in many forecasting or predictive studies.

While the sample size issue is almost always discussed in terms of experimental research and theory validation studies, this issue is of equal importance to school administrators and policymakers who wish to make more effective use of decision-oriented research to improve classroom instruction and the administration of schools. Specifically, correct sample sizes are essential for producing valid evidence that documents the success of school intervention programs. Correct sample sizes are also required to obtain accurate information in needs assessments, student enrollment projections, policy preference surveys, and cost effectiveness studies.

The intent of this chapter is to illustrate that the problems encountered in choosing an appropriate sample size in school improvement research projects can be significantly reduced by designating at the outset exactly how the sampling information will be used to guide both data analysis and the interpretation of findings.

Statisticians and sampling theorists (Babbie, 1990; Kirk, 1984; Shavelson, 1988; Williams, 1978) have indicated that probability samples are used in statistical inference for two primary purposes: (1) to estimate population parameters and (2) to test research hypotheses about one or more populations of interest.

Once researchers have specified the primary purpose of their study, two standard, but different, basic strategies are readily available to determine the appropriate sample size requirements.

With these strategies in mind, the chapter is divided into two parts. The first part describes the basic parameter estimation strategy and the second elaborates the strategy used in hypothesis testing. Each part contains case studies to illustrate how and when these two strategies should be used.

PART ONE: PARAMETER ESTIMATION STUDIES

The primary intent of many surveys or exploratory studies is to make inferences about a population of interest on the basis of information obtained in a sample from that population. Inferences in these investigations are usually aimed at the *estimation* of certain numerical characteristics of the population such as a mean, proportion, total or variance. These numerical descriptive measures of the population are called *parameters*.

The numerical descriptive measures of a sample are called *statistics* or *estimators,* and are usually accompanied by error of estimation indicators that assess the magnitude of error associated with using a sample rather than a complete count of population elements.

In most surveys or polls, the error of estimate indicator is called a *margin of error.* Typically, this margin of error is three percent in national polls and four or five percent in smaller-scale surveys such as those conducted by school districts (see Note 1).

These features of an estimation study are illustrated in two case studies. Both illustrations are based on a school district's desire to conduct a policy preference survey. Case One will use a simple random sampling design and Case Two will use a stratified random sampling design.

For the record, the use of the term *simple* in Case One implies that the required sample will be selected randomly from a single list containing all members in the population of interest.

The use of the term *stratified* in Case Two implies that the list of all members in the population will be used to create two or more separate lists. Each list is then treated as a separate simple random sample. In this design, estimates are first given for each group (stratum) and then combined across groups (strata) to provide a single estimate for the entire population (see Note 2).

Case One: A Simple Random Sampling Design

An urban school district planning committee is considering a year-round schooling program. Let us assume that the members of this planning group wish to estimate the percent of the district's 1,000 classroom teachers who would prefer to explore the year-round school alternative.

Given this interest, the questionnaire item for the preference survey might be the following: *This school district is considering a year-round school program. Would you prefer this alternative to our existing nine-month school year? (Yes or No).*

Sampling Design

An appropriate survey sampling design for Case One is a simple random sampling design. To implement this basic probability sampling design, one would begin by constructing a list of all classroom teachers in the district. Numbering the entries in this teacher list would reveal the size of the population (N).

Once N is known, a published sampling table (for example see Krejcie and Morgan, 1970) can be consulted to indicate the required sample size (n). Finally, a table of random numbers or a computerized random number generator can be used to select n random numbers between one and N. Teachers whose numbers were selected would then be asked to respond to the survey question specified above.

When all n respondents have indicated their preferences, the proportion of *yes* respondents identified in sample data (p) would provide the estimate of true proportion (P) of all classroom teachers who prefer the year-round school alternative.

Sampling Tables

An abbreviated (but typical) simple random sampling table is given in Table 4.1. Its interpretation is straightforward. For example, if a school district has 200 classroom teachers, the required sample size in Table 4.1 is 132. Thus, **N** is 200 and **n** is 132, which represents 66 percent of the classroom teacher population.

If the school district of interest in our case study was a very large urban school district, then **N** might be 5,000. For this school district, the required sample size in Table 4.1 is **n** equal to 357. In this case, the sample size is just 7.14 percent of the population.

A careful examination of Table 4.1 clearly indicates the efficiency of probability sampling. Specifically, the larger the population, the smaller the percent of the population needed in the sample. Moreover, the *maximum* sample size for any population—no matter how large it is—is just 384.

Table 4.1. Typical table for determining sample size.

Population (**N**)	Sample (**n**)	Sample Percent of Population 100(**n/N**)
50	44	88.00
100	80	80.00
200	132	66.00
500	217	43.40
1,000	**278**	**27.80**
5,000	357	7.14
10,000	370	3.70
20,000	377	1.89
75,000	382	0.51
1,000,000	384	0.04
2,000,000	384	0.02
4,000,000	384	0.01

Note: This table is an abbreviated version of a typical published sample size table for a simple random sampling design. Table is constructed to yield a 95 percent confidence interval for a margin of error not to exceed 5 percent. It assumes no reliable prior information is known about the true proportion of yes responses in the population of interest. For all populations having more than four million members, the required sample size (**n**) will be 384 and the sample percent of the population will always be less than 0.01, the last entry in column three above.

Returning to Case One, the actual classroom teacher population is **N** equal to 1,000. Using Table 4.1 the required sample size is **n** equal to 278 which represents 27.8 percent of the total population of classroom teachers in the district. Accordingly, 278 randomly selected classroom teachers would be requested to complete the district's questionnaire and these 278 responses would be used to estimate the true proportion of all classroom teachers in the district who prefer the year-round school program.

Sample Size

The use of a typical published sample size table to determine the required sample size for Case One involves agreement with three preprogrammed decision rules. The three preprogrammed decisions, the symbols used to represent them, and the actual preset decision rule values are as follows:

1. *The confidence value* (**A**) has been preset at 3.84 to indicate the use of a 95 percent confidence interval for reporting the margin of error.

2. *The precision value* (**B**) has been preset at 0.05 to guarantee a margin of error no larger than 5 percent.

3. *The prior information value* (**P**) has been preset at 0.50 to indicate that there is no reliable presurvey estimate of the true proportion of *yes* responses in the population of interest, which in this case study is all 1,000 classroom teachers in the district.

Table 4.2 is used to illustrate how these decision rules are addressed in a step-by-step procedure that yields the required sample size for the simple random sampling design used in Case One. Notice that the three decision rules are specified in steps one through three. Once these specifications are in place, step four in Table 4.2 is used to consult the appropriate sampling table to specify the required sample size.

Strategies to reduce the required sample size can be explored by using different decision rule values for **A**, **B** and **P** in the first

Table 4.2. Procedures for determining the Case One sample size.

Step One: Specify the confidence level value (A).

Decision Rule One: Set **A** at 3.84. This specification indicates the use of a 95 confidence interval for reporting the margin of error.

Step Two: Specify the precision value (B).

Decision Rule Two: Set **B** at 0.05. This specification guarantees a margin of error no larger than 5 percent.

Step Three: Specify the prior information value (P).

Decision Rule Three: Set **P** at 0.50. This specification indicates that there is no reliable presurvey estimate of the true proportion of yes responses in the population under study.

Step Four: Select required sample size from sampling table.

Given the three decision rules specified above, the simple random sampling design used in the Case One policy preference survey would require a sample size of 278 classroom teachers.

---

three steps of Table 4.2. These strategies are elaborated in McNamara (1978 and 1992a).

For the purpose of this article, it is important to note just one thing: *The required sample size in an estimation study using a probability sampling plan can be determined only after all three decision rule values are specified.*

Estimation Procedures

For every sample size table, there is a second table that is used to indicate the actual margin of error that results from the analysis of the survey responses. Table 4.3 is the corresponding table for Case One where **N** is 1,000 and **n** is 278. Consistent with the decision rules specified in Table 4.2, the survey findings are to be reported using a 95 percent confidence interval for the margin of error.

Table 4.3 also has a straightforward interpretation. If the actual percent of *yes* responses for this classroom teacher survey is 55 percent, then we take the position that the correct percent for the population that includes all classroom teachers in the district is between 50 percent and 60 percent (see Note 3). While only one percentage value will result from conducting a survey, it is important to recognize that the actual sample percent of *yes* responses can be any value between zero and 100. Thus, **p,** the corresponding sample proportion, could range from zero to one.

Table 4.3 is constructed to cover all of these possibilities. For example, if the actual percent of *yes* responses for the classroom teachers in the sample is 85 percent, the margin of error would be 3.6 percent and the 95 percent confidence interval to estimate the true percent of *yes* responses for the Case One classroom teacher population would range from 81.4 percent to 88.6 percent.

A careful examination of Table 4.3 exhibits a very important sampling design consequence. Specifically, the margin of error for implementing the simple random sampling design where **N**

Table 4.3. Precision values for possible Case One sample results.

Sample Proportion (p)	Sample Percent (100 p)	Margin of Error (%)	Confidence Interval Low (%)	Confidence Interval High (%)
0.50	50	5.0	45.0	55.0
0.55	**55**	**5.0**	**50.0**	**60.0**
0.60	60	4.9	55.1	64.9
0.65	65	4.8	60.2	69.8
0.70	70	4.6	65.4	74.6
0.75	75	4.3	70.7	79.3
0.80	80	4.0	76.0	84.0
0.85	85	3.6	81.4	88.6
0.90	90	3.0	87.0	93.0
0.95	95	2.2	92.8	97.2
0.99	99	1.0	98.0	100.0

Note: Table was constructed for a simple random sample of 278 from a population of 1,000 using the procedures detailed in McNamara (1992a). Entries can be interpreted as follows. If the sample percent of yes responses is 55 percent, the margin of error is 5 percent and the 95 percent confidence interval for the true proportion of yes responses in the population is between 50 percent and 60 percent. For sample values less than 50 percent, use the same distance above 50 percent. For example, if the sample percent is 10 percent, use the 90 percent entry. In this case, the margin of error is 3 percent and the 95 percent confidence interval ranges from a low of 7 percent ot a high of 13 percent.

is 1,000 and **n** is 278 will *never* exceed 5 percent. However, as the actual percent of *yes* responses in the sample increases beyond 50 percent, the corresponding margin of error decreases (see Note 4).

Case Two: A Stratified Random Sampling Design

The second case study is a reconsideration of the initial estimation problem addressed in Case One. For Case Two, let us assume again that a school district's planning committee is considering a year-round schooling program. As before, members of this planning group wish to estimate the percent of the district's 1,000 classroom teachers who would prefer to explore the year-round school alternative.

In addition to estimating just the overall percent of all classroom teachers who would prefer the year-round school alternative, let us assume the planning group would also like to estimate both the percent of its 400 elementary school teachers and the percent of its 600 secondary school classroom teachers who prefer the year-round school alternative.

The planning group believes this additional estimation information would be of help to them in designing a single school district pilot study at either the elementary or the secondary level. Specifically, the district's planning committee wishes to use these two additional estimates to select for the pilot study the classroom teacher group most likely to support the year-round school program.

Given these information needs, the Case Two questionnaire item in the district's preference survey would be identical to the questionnaire item used in Case One (see Note 5).

Sampling Design

An appropriate survey sampling design for Case Two is a stratified random sampling design. To implement this basic probability sampling design, one would begin by securing a list of all 1,000 classroom teachers in the district. Thus, the size of total population of interest is $N(T)$ equal to 1,000.

Next, two separate lists would be constructed. The first list would contain the names of all 400 elementary school classroom teachers in the district. The population size of this group (stratum) would be **N(E)** equal to 400. Accordingly, the elementary school teacher population would represent 40 percent of the total teacher population, a fact we will need to solve the sample size problem.

Similarly, the second list would contain the names of all secondary school teachers. The population size of this group (stratum) would be **N(S)** equal to 600. Thus, the secondary school teacher population would represent 60 percent of the total teacher population **N(T)**.

Both the selection of sample sizes and the estimation of the three parameters of interest to the district's planning committee are discussed below.

What should be kept in mind at this point is one key point; namely, the same three basic decision rules used in Case One are needed to determine the required sample sizes for Case Two. In addition, a fourth decision rule is needed to account for the stratification feature in the sampling plan.

Sample Sizes

The four decision rules needed to determine the two required group sample sizes for Case Two are elaborated in Table 4.4.

Careful inspection of this table indicates that the first two decision rule values for the stratified random sampling design are identical to those used in Case One. Specifically, these two decision rule specifications reflect the planning committee's request to have a 95 percent confidence interval (see **A** in step one) and a margin of error no larger than 5 percent (see **B** in step two) for estimating **P(T)**, the proportion of all 1,000 classroom teachers who prefer the year-round school alternative.

The third decision rule specification is given in step three of Table 4.4. This specification indicates that there is no prior information for either **P(E)**, the true proportion of *yes* responses for all 400 elementary school classroom teachers, or for **P(S)**, the true proportion of *yes* responses for all secondary school classroom teachers.

While the third step of Table 4.4 also focuses on the basic prior information concern, it is important to note that two specific

Table 4.4. Procedures for determining the Case Two sample sizes.

Step One: Specify the confidence level value (A).

Decision Rule One: Set **A** at 3.84. This specification indicates the use of a 95 percent confidence interval for reporting the margin of error.

Step Two: Specify the precision value (B).

Decision Rule Two: Set **B** at 0.05. This specification guarantees a margin of error no larger than 5 percent.

Step Three: Specify the prior information value (P) for each group.

Decision Rule Three: Set **P(E)** and **P(S)** at 0.50. This specification indicates that there is no reliable presurvey estimate of the true proportion of yes responses for either the subpopulation of elementary level teachers **P(E)** or the subpopulation of secondary level teachers **P(S)**.

Step Four: Indicate the allocation plan for the sampling design.

Decision Rule Four: Declare a proportional allocation plan. This decision indicates that the proportion of the sample size for each group (stratum) will be identical to the proportion of the total population residing in that group.

Step Five: Select the total required sample size (n).

Given the four decision rules specified above, the stratified random sampling design used in the Case Two policy preference survey would require a total sample size (**n**) of 278 classroom teachers.

Step Six: Determine the required sample size for each group.

Given that 40 percent of the population are elementary school classroom teachers and 60 percent are secondary school classroom teachers, the required sample size for the elementary school classroom teacher group is 40 percent of **n**, which equals 111, and the required sample size for the secondary classroom is 60 percent of **n**, which equals 167.

---

decision values are required, one for each stratum used in the stratification plan. Recall, only one prior information specification was needed in the simple random sampling design used in Case One (see step three in Table 4.2).

Switching from the simple random sampling design to the stratified random sampling design also requires a specification for a fourth decision rule. This additional specification is given in step four of Table 4.4.

The fourth decision rule is used to specify how the total required sample size $n(T)$ needed to estimate $P(T)$ will be allocated to the two separate groups (strata) used in the survey sampling design.

Statistically speaking, the fourth decision rule is needed for two reasons. First, it is needed for the formula (or sampling table) used to determine the overall required sample size $n(T)$. This need is addressed in step five of Table 4.4 (see Note 6).

Second, the fourth decision rule specification is also needed to determine the required sample sizes for both $n(E)$ and $n(S)$, the two strata used in Case Two. This task is addressed in step six of Table 4.4.

Since a proportional allocation was specified in step four, you will notice that the two proportions of classroom teachers in the total sample are *identical* to the two proportions of classroom teachers in the total population.

Specifically, the required elementary school sample size $n(E)$ is designated to be 40 percent of the total sample size $n(T)$. Also, the total elementary school teacher population size $N(E)$ is 40 percent of the total teacher population $N(T)$. Similarly, $n(S)$ is designated to be 60 percent of $n(T)$ and $N(S)$ is 60 percent of $N(T)$.

With these four decision rules from Table 4.4 in place, the stratified random sampling design formulas for proportional allocation yield these three solutions. First, $n(T)$ is equal to 278. Second, $n(E)$ is 40 percent of 278 which is 111. Third, $n(S)$ is 60 percent of 278 which is 167 (see Note 7).

Estimation Procedures

The corresponding estimation table for the stratified random sampling design implemented in Case Two is given in Table 4.5. Its purpose is to produce the best estimate for $P(T)$, the true proportion of all classroom teachers in the district who prefer the year-round school alternative.

Four specific values are needed to estimate $P(T)$. These are defined in the table legend. Their contributions to determining $p(T)$, the sample estimator of the parameter $P(T)$, are given in the Table 4.5 formula.

Table 4.5. The estimation model for Case Two.

Formula
p(T) = S(E) × p(E) + S(S) × p(S)

Legend
p(T) = the survey estimate of the true proportion of all of the school district's class-room teachers who prefer the year-round school alternative.
p(E) = the survey estimate of the true proportion of all elementary school classroom teachers who prefer the year-round school alternative.
p(S) = the survey estimate of the true proportion of all secondary school classroom teachers who prefer the year-round school alternative.
S(E) = the proportion of all classroom teachers in the school district who are elementary school teachers.
S(S) = the proportion of all classroom teachers in the school district who are secondary school teachers.

To illustrate how the estimation model is applied to the actual sample results, let us assume that **p(E)**, the sample estimate of **P(E)**, is 0.35 and **p(S)**, the sample estimate of **P(T)**, is 0.75.

This assumption about the actual survey results implies that 35 percent of the elementary school teachers in the sample and 75 percent of the secondary school teachers in the sample gave *yes* responses to reflect their preferences for the year-round school alternative.

These assumptions about the actual survey responses are entered into the estimation model illustration given in Table 4.6 along with **S(E)** and **S(S)**, which are the two sample proportions discussed earlier in the treatment of sample size requirements.

These results suggest three conclusions to be considered by the school district planning committee.

First, the best estimate of the percent of all 1,000 classroom teachers in the school district who favor the year-round school alternative is 59 percent.

Second, the true percent of all classroom teachers in the school district who favor the year-round school program is between 54.5 percent and 63.5 percent. Thus, the school district's planning committee should be confident in stating that a majority of all classroom teachers in the school district (approximately three out of every five) prefer year-round schools to their existing school schedule (see Note 8).

Third, secondary school classroom teachers (75 percent) are more likely than elementary school classroom teachers (35 percent) to favor the year-round school program. Thus, the school district's planning committee should conduct its pilot program at the secondary level if it wishes to begin its exploratory efforts with classroom teachers who are most likely to be advocates of year-round schools (see Note 9).

Resources for Solving Estimation Problems

In general, sample size procedures for any of the four common survey sampling designs used to solve parameter estimation problems (simple random sampling, stratified random sampling,

Table 4.6. Application of the Case Two estimation model.

Input Values
p(E) = 0.35, which indicates that 35 percent of the elementary school classroom teachers prefer the year-round school alternative.
p(S) = 0.75, which indicates that 75 percent of the secondary school classroom teachers prefer the year-round school alternative.
S(E) = 0.40, because 400 of the 1,000 classroom teachers in the school district are elementary school teachers.
S(S) = 0.60, because 600 of the 1,000 classroom teachers in the school district are secondary school teachers.

Estimation Model Results
p(T) = S(E) × p(E) + S(S) × p(S)   p(T) = (0.40) × (0.35) + (0.60) × (0.75) = 0.59

Interpretation
Point Estimate—Given a p(T) value equal to 0.59 indicates that the best estimate of the true percent of all 1,000 classroom teachers in the school district P(T) who prefer the year-round school alternative to the existing nine-month school year is 59 percent.
Confidence Interval—The margin of error for using p(T) to estimate the true proportion P(T) is 0.045. Accordingly, the survey results indicate we are 95 percent certain that the true proportion of all 1,000 classroom teachers in the school district who prefer the year-round school alternative is between 54.5 percent and 63.5 percent.

cluster sampling and systematic sampling) follow the procedures provided in the two case problems elaborated previously.

Researchers and administrators in search of a practical guide detailing specific solution techniques for these estimation problems will need to look beyond traditional educational research methods and basic behavioral science statistics texts. Specifically, these texts almost always concentrate their efforts on elaborating statistical models and solution techniques for testing hypotheses associated with well-structured experiments or straightforward comparisons. Moreover, when stratified and cluster sampling are discussed in educational research texts, the treatment of these two most common survey sampling design options is usually restricted to verbal descriptions of their availability and relevance.

For most school improvement research projects, the search for a practical guide detailing specific solution techniques for estimation problems can be found in Scheaffer, Mendenhall and Ott (1990). This source provides a rich resource for practitioners as well as for research and evaluation specialists. It includes a wide array of realistic case studies and the corresponding solution techniques for determining the correct sample sizes based on the three decision rules specified above for the confidence value (**A**), the precision value (**B**) and the prior information value (**P**).

Those who wish to learn more about basic procedures for reducing required sample sizes in estimation studies used in school improvement research are encouraged to review McNamara (1978 and 1992a). These two sources illustrate how making small changes in one or more of the three decision rules for **A**, **B** and **P** can yield substantial reductions in the required sample sizes needed to estimate policy planning parameters.

PART TWO: HYPOTHESIS TESTING STUDIES

In many educational research investigations, the primary interest of the inquiry is not to estimate parameters, but rather to test research hypotheses for one or more populations of interest. The hypothesis testing problem is frequently encountered in both theory and practice.

A good example of a theoretical inquiry in educational research is a study of work-related attitudes and behaviors conducted by Hollon and Gemmill (1976). These organizational theorists used a t test for two independent sample means to test four major research hypotheses that predicted female teaching professionals, in comparison to their male counterparts, would experience (1) less perceived participation in decision making, (2) greater job-related tension, (3) less job involvement, and (4) less overall job satisfaction.

A more recent theoretical inquiry that used the same basic t test is a study by Papalewis, Bushman and Brown (1989). These investigators used research hypotheses to advance the idea that teachers and school administrators would offer different responses on twelve criterion measures that reflect the perceived organizational culture of their school district (see Note 10).

In practice, the hypothesis testing problem is encountered in school improvement research experiments where school administrators wish to compare the effectiveness of new or promising intervention strategies (experimental methods) with current instructional practices (traditional methods). This problem is also encountered in nonexperimental school district studies when administrators and policy makers wish to compare different student, teacher, or parent groups on a criterion variable of interest.

When hypothesis testing rather than parameter estimation is the primary focus of an investigation, a different set of decision rules must be specified to guide decisions regarding sample size. Once these hypothesis testing decision rules are specified by the investigator, standard statistical formulas are readily available to determine the required sample sizes.

This decision rule strategy is illustrated below in two school improvement research case studies. Case Three addresses hypothesis testing in an experimental study. Case Four treats hypothesis testing in a nonexperimental situation where there is a need to verify teacher differences toward a policy of interest to a school district.

For the purpose of this article, just one important idea should be kept in mind during the review of these two cases: *The required sample sizes in a hypothesis testing study using a probabil-*

*ity sampling plan can be determined only after four decision rule
values are specified.*

Case Three: An Experimental Design

Following the recommendations reported in the new National
Council of Teachers of Mathematics standards for improving
mathematics in elementary and secondary schools (Ball and
Schroeder, 1992), a large urban school district decided that one of
the primary goals it wished to pursue was improving student
performance in senior high school mathematics. Accordingly, a
district task force was formed to investigate how this might be
done.

After conducting an intensive fact-finding effort, the task force
decided its first goal should be to improve teaching and learning
in its Algebra I classes. They believed that this initial goal was
an essential first step and one likely to directly influence future
efforts to improve more advanced mathematics courses offered in
the district.

With this shared goal in mind, the school district's task force is
in an excellent position to undertake a school improvement research project. Three specific tasks are involved in this project.

The first task for this action research group would be to locate
a more effective strategy for teaching Algebra I courses. Let us
assume that this task has been completed and the district's task
force is convinced that teaching Algebra I using the problem
solving and graphic method (Kysh, 1991) will increase student
achievement in Algebra I.

The second task for this action research group would be to conduct a fair test that compares the performance of the district's
Algebra I students exposed to the new experimental teaching
method with those who are taught Algebra I using the traditional method (the method used in prior years). The typical
length of time for a valid comparative experiment such as this
one would be a single school year.

The third task for this group would be to evaluate the results
of the district's experiment. A careful evaluation of student performance results would clearly support (or fail to support) the

task force's belief that the new method of teaching Algebra I is more effective in their school district. Depending on the actual experimental outcomes, the task force could recommend (or not recommend) that the school district adopt the new method in all Algebra I classes.

Research Design

An overview of how this comparative experiment would proceed is given in Table 4.7. Notice that the experiment is guided by a single research hypothesis. For the record, it should be stated that research hypotheses are theoretical statements (informed conjectures or educated guesses) about an expected difference or an expected relationship. They are not statistical statements, and they do not need to be put in null form.

The experimental results for Case Three are entered in Table 4.7. This outcome measure reflects a summary of results (means and standard deviations) for the two sample groups on a standardized Algebra I examination known to have an excellent content validity in terms of the district's Algebra I curriculum guide.

Since the Table 4.7 results were obtained from two experimental samples, they are called statistics. For example, the sample mean $M(1)$ is a statistic because it is a summary measure based on all the Algebra I test scores for students in the experiment exposed to Method One. As a statistic, $M(1)$ is an unbiased estimate for $\mu(1)$, a parameter reflecting what the mean would have been if the entire school district Algebra I student population were taught using only Method One.

Similarly, $M(2)$ is also a statistic. It provides an estimate for $\mu(2)$, a second parameter of interest that reflects the typical student performance when only Method Two is used throughout the district.

Hence, $\mu(1)$ and $\mu(2)$ are parameters that reflect two different policy options available to the school district. From a policy research perspective, the fair-test experiment is a practical one because it models exactly the two actual policy options under investigation by the district's task force.

Table 4.7. The experimental design for Case Three.

Research Hypothesis: The experimental method (#1) is more effective than the traditional method (#2).

Verification Strategy: Design and conduct a true experiment to verify the claim made in the research hypothesis.

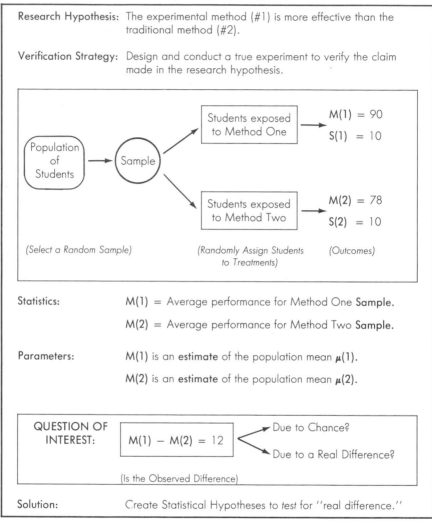

(Select a Random Sample)   (Randomly Assign Students   (Outcomes)
                                   to Treatments)

Statistics: M(1) = Average performance for Method One **Sample.**

                         M(2) = Average performance for Method Two **Sample.**

Parameters: M(1) is an **estimate** of the population mean $\mu(1)$.

                         M(2) is an **estimate** of the population mean $\mu(2)$.

QUESTION OF
INTEREST: $M(1) - M(2) = 12$ ⟶ Due to Chance?

                                                   ⟶ Due to a Real Difference?

                       (Is the Observed Difference)

Solution: Create Statistical Hypotheses to *test* for ''real difference.''

The big question to be addressed in the inferential model elaborated in Table 4.7 is to determine if the observed sample mean difference of 12 points is more likely to be *due to chance* (happened only because of sampling error) or *due to real difference* (one method is actually more effective).

It is at this point in the analysis of experimental data that one becomes interested in statistical hypotheses and statistical inference. Specifically, in the logic of hypothesis testing, statistical hypotheses and probability theory can be used to help the decision maker reach an informed decision about the actual sample mean difference encountered in the experiment.

Statistical Inference

In making statistical inferences, Shavelson (1988) suggests that the researcher assumes the role of a decision maker. The decision issue is to reject or fail to reject the null statistical hypothesis indicating no difference.

For the Algebra I case study, the correct null statistical hypothesis is given in step one in Table 4.8. The symbol for this hypothesis is **H(0).**

To be absolutely certain about reaching a correct decision, a researcher would have to measure every person in the population. In many school improvement research studies, this certainty requirement is impractical.

Accordingly, the researcher usually operates under conditions of uncertainty and draws a random sample from the population of interest (see Table 4.7). Using data from the random sample and a test statistic, the researcher infers what is true of the population. Based on these test results, the researcher decides whether or not to reject the null statistical hypothesis. This procedure is illustrated in Table 4.8.

Decision Problem

Whenever researchers use sample data to estimate a population difference, there is always some degree of uncertainty about whether the difference of the sample means accurately reflects the true population difference. Hence, researchers must make an inference from sample data to decide whether or not a true difference exists.

This decision problem can be seen in Table 4.7. Notice again that two alternatives exist for the 12 point difference en-

Table 4.8. Hypotheses and decision rules for Case Three.

Step One: Indicate the statistical hypotheses

Null Hypothesis	H(0):	$\mu(1)$ equals $\mu(2)$
Alternative Hypothesis	H(A):	$\mu(1)$ is *not* equal to $\mu(2)$

H(0) is a statistical null hypothesis indicating that the two methods of teaching Algebra I are equally effective.

H(A) is a statistical alternative hypothesis indicating that the two methods of teaching Algebra I are *not* equally effective.

$\mu(1)$ is a parameter indicating the mean performance score for the district's Algebra I student population when all students are taught using Method One.

$\mu(2)$ is a parameter indicating the mean performance score for the district's Algebra I student population when all students are taught using Method Two.

Step Two: Specify the decision rules for evaluating H(0)

Reject H(0) if the effect size value observed exceeds **0.50**

Retain H(0) if the effect size value observed does *not* exceed **0.50**

Step Three: Calculate the test statistic for the experiment

The essential input information needed to calculate the observed effect size for the two independent samples is as follows:

- Sample mean for Method One is **90**.
- Sample mean for Method Two is **78**.
- Sample mean difference is **12**.
- Common standard deviation is **10**.

Inserting this information into the effect size formula, the observed test statistic value for this experiment is **1.2**.

Step Four: Indicate the decision regarding H(0)

The observed effect size value of **1.2** exceeds the decision rule effect size value of **0.50** specified in step two above. Thus, H(0) is rejected and a meaningful significant difference favoring Method One is detected.

Step Five: Interpret the statistical test findings

Given a meaningful significant difference favoring Method One, the researcher would conclude that Method One was a more effective method for teaching Algebra I in the district where the experiment was conducted.

countered in the Algebra I case study experiment. This difference could be due to chance (happened only because of sampling error) or due to a real difference (one teaching method is actually more effective).

This decision problem has two features. First, there is the true situation in the population. Second, there is a need to infer the true situation from the sample data. This decision problem can be put into the familiar hypothesis testing model for comparing the results from two independent samples.

This has been done for the Algebra I case study in Table 4.8. In step one, the researcher formulates two statistical hypotheses. $H(0)$ in Table 4.8 equates $\mu(1)$ to $\mu(2)$.

This null hypothesis suggests that the two parameters (population values) are equal, implying that any observed difference in the two samples is due only to chance. Thus, $H(0)$ for this experiment places the two parameters in an equation to infer that the two Algebra I teaching methods are equally effective.

Since $H(0)$ might not be true, the researcher needs to specify an alternative statistical hypothesis. Accordingly, step one in Table 4.8 specifies $H(A)$, an alternative statistical hypothesis which fits this logical requirement. Note that $H(0)$ and $H(A)$ are complementary. This implies that they have no overlap and between them they exhaust all possible outcomes of the experiment (see Note 11).

Correct Decisions

In the population, $H(0)$ is either true or false. When the sample data are linked with the decision rule (see step two in Table 4.8), the researcher may decide to reject or not to reject $H(0)$. This decision could be correct or incorrect. This decision situation is depicted in Table 4.9.

A careful examination of Table 4.9 indicates that researchers can make correct decisions when they decide (a) to *not* reject a true null hypothesis or (b) to reject a false null hypothesis. These two correct decision possibilities are labeled Case 1 and Case 4.

Table 4.9. The decision problem in hypothesis testing.

		H(0) IS TRUE	H(0) IS FALSE
Decision alternatives based on inferences from sample data	DO NOT REJECT H(0)	Correct Decision *Case 1*	Incorrect Decision Type II Error *Case 2*
	REJECT H(0)	Incorrect Decision Type I Error *Case 3*	Correct Decision *Case 4*

Interpretation:

Statistical Hypothesis. H(0) is the null statistical hypothesis. For two independent samples, H(0) declares that the true population means (parameters) for the two groups under investigation are equal. Hence, H(0) implies that there is no difference in the two groups.

Logical Errors. Since the true population is not known, researchers use data from random samples and a statistical test to infer what is true in the population of interest. This inferential decision-making process must guard against two possible errors. These are Type I errors (see Case 3) and Type II errors (see Case 2).

Actual Error. Once a specific statistical test of H(0) is conducted, only one correct or incorrect decision is possible. Thus, only one actual error occurs each time an inferential decision is made. Specifically,

When the researcher's inferential decision results in not rejecting H(0), there are only two possibilities.

If H(0) is true in the population, a **correct** decision was made (see Case 1).

If H(0) is false in the population, an **incorrect** decision was made, resulting in a Type II Error (see Case 2).

When the researcher's inferential decision results in rejecting H(0), there are only two possibilities.

If H(0) is true in the population, an **incorrect** decision was made, resulting in a Type I Error (see Case 3).

If H(0) is false in the population, a **correct** decision was made (see Case 4).

Decision Strategy. Since the true situation in the population of interest is not known, researchers should use random samples and statistical tests that minimize the probability of committing either type of inferential error.

Incorrect Decisions

Table 4.9 also indicates that researchers can make two types of errors. A *Type I Error* occurs when researchers incorrectly reject a true null hypothesis. This possibility is given in Case 3.

Researchers can make another type of error in situations where the null hypothesis is false. Specifically, a *Type II Error* occurs when researchers incorrectly fail to reject (do *not* reject) a false null hypothesis. This possibility is given in Case 2 in Table 4.9.

Logical Versus Actual Errors

While the decision problem charted in Table 4.9 specifies two logical errors, only one of these two types of errors can occur in testing a specific null hypothesis.

This can be illustrated using Table 4.9. If the application of the effect size decision rule (specified in step two in Table 4.8) leads the researcher to reject H(0), only the bottom row of Table 4.9 needs to be examined. If H(0) is true in the population, an incorrect decision was made (see Case 3). If H(0) is false in the population, a correct decision was made (see Case 4).

On the other hand, if the effect size decision rule leads the researcher to *not* reject (retain) II(0), then only the top row of Table 4.9 would be examined. Once again, there would be only one correct decision (see Case 1) and one incorrect decision (see Case 2).

Since statistical decision makers must operate under conditions of uncertainty, applications of statistical inference must be concerned with both types of errors. This concern can be expressed in terms of error probabilities that accurately reflect the risk of committing either a Type I or Type II error.

Alpha

To avoid a Type I error, researchers frequently set the level of statistical significance at 0.05. In inferential terms, the level of significance is called alpha.

The precise inferential specification is as follows: the probability of committing a Type I error is alpha. This specification emphasizes the distinction between a Type I error as a logical consideration and alpha as a probability specified in the inferential model to cover this logical possibility.

Beta

To avoid a Type II error, researchers should (but seldom do) specify a predetermined probability to cover this potential error. In inferential terms, this probability is called beta.

Similarly, the precise inferential specification is stated as follows: the probability of committing a Type II error is called beta. Once again, this expression helps to distinguish between a Type II error as a logical possibility and beta as a predetermined probability to cover this inferential error.

Four Essential Probabilities

It must be kept in mind that the true situation in the population is not known by the researcher. Accordingly, four probabilities are operating each time one tests a hypothesis about a difference in the population using sample data and a test statistic. Two of these probabilities are alpha and beta. The other two probabilities are associated with making a correct decision and can be expressed as complements to alpha and beta.

The probability of correctly retaining $H(0)$ when it is true in the population is one minus alpha. The probability of correctly rejecting $H(0)$ is one minus beta. The formal name of this probability is statistical power (see Note 12).

All four of these probabilities and their influence on the decision about retaining or rejecting $H(0)$ are summarized in the top half of Table 4.10.

The best strategy for guarding against either type of error in a proposed sampling design is to specify *low* probabilities for both alpha and beta. Moreover, if a researcher believes it is equally important to guard against Type I and Type II errors, equal *low* probabilities should be specified for both alpha and beta.

Table 4.10. Four probabilities specified in hypothesis testing.

Since the true situation in the population is not known by the researcher, four probabilities are operating each time a researcher tests a hypothesis about a true difference in the population using sample data and a test statistic. These are: Probability of incorrectly rejecting a true H(0) = Alpha.   Probability of correctly retaining a true H(0) = 1 − Alpha.   Probability of incorrectly retaining a false H(0) = Beta.   Probability of correctly rejecting a false H(0) = 1 − Beta.   H(0) is a statistical null hypothesis specifying no difference in the population. Its truth is unknown to the researcher.
In practice, a researcher specifies the two error probabilities which are alpha and beta. In the Algebra I case study example, both alpha and beta were set at 0.05. Accordingly, the four exact probabilities for testing the hypothesis about a difference between the two teaching methods were: Probability of incorrectly rejecting a true H(0) = 0.05.   Probability of correctly retaining a true H(0) = (1 − 0.05) = 0.95.   Probability of incorrectly retaining a false H(0) = 0.05.   Probability of correctly rejecting a false H(0) = (1 − 0.05) = 0.95.   The statistical null hypothesis in this case study indicates that there is no difference in the effectiveness of the two teaching methods. Its truth is unknown to the researcher.

Sample Sizes

With this sampling design strategy in mind, one can proceed to determine the two required sample sizes for the Algebra I experiment in Case Three. Four specific decision rules must be addressed to make this determination. These four decision rules are given in the first four steps of Table 4.11. The following is a review of each of these five steps.

In step one, alpha was set at 0.05. This error probability acknowledges that the risk of a Type I error is five percent.

In step two, beta was also set at 0.05. This error probability acknowledges that the risk of a Type II error is also five percent.

Since alpha and beta were both set at 0.05, the researcher is clearly indicating that it is equally important to guard against each type of error.

All four of the probabilities resulting from the specifications given in these first two steps are entered in the bottom half of

Table 4.11. Procedure for determining the Case Three sample sizes.

Step One: Specify alpha to minimize the risk of a Type I error. Decision Rule One: Set alpha at 0.05. Step Two: Specify beta to minimize the risk of a Type II error. Decision Rule Two: Set beta at 0.05. Step Three: Indicate the type of alternative statistical hypothesis. Decision Rule Three: Declare a nondirectional alternative statistical hypothesis to be used in the hypothesis testing model. Step Four: Declare the desired effect size criterion. Decision Rule Four: Set the effect size at 0.50. Step Five: Select required sample size from sampling table. Given the four decision rules specified above, the random sampling design used in the experiment would require a total sample size of 210 with two equal samples of 105 each. Since beta is 0.05 in the second decision rule, the statistical power is 0.95.

Table 4.10. Note that setting beta at 0.05 also indicates that the desired statistical power for the proposed sampling design is equal to 0.95.

In step three, a nondirectional alternative statistical hypothesis was specified. This hypothesis allows **H(0)** to be rejected if a real difference favoring either group is detected (see Note 13).

Step four in Table 4.11 was used to specify a desired effect size equal to 0.50.

An effect size is a statistical indicator that takes the form of a ratio. Its numerator is the difference between the two population means. Its denominator is the population (common) standard deviation.

An effect size of 0.50 implies that the two population means under study differ by one-half a population standard deviation.

Specification of an effect size decision rule prior to conducting a fair-test experiment provides a straightforward way (an operational definition) to distinguish between statistically significant differences that are trivial and statistically significant differences that are meaningful.

This decision rule (which was also entered in step two of Table 4.8) acknowledges that the case study school district would be willing to adopt the new Algebra I teaching method in all senior high schools if the fair-test experiment had an actual effect size equal to or greater than 0.50 favoring Method One (see Note 14). Practically speaking, declaring an effect size of 0.50 means the school district would invest in Method One if it demonstrated that an additional 19 percent (or more) of its Algebra I students had better performance scores when taught by Method One rather than Method Two.

Finally, step five in Table 4.11 is used to determine the minimum sample sizes needed to ensure a statistical power equal to 0.95. These minimum sample sizes were located in a published sample size table using all four essential decision rules given in the four previous steps. *If any one of the four essential decision rules is not specified, the published sample size tables can not be used.*

Sample size tables for a statistical test involving two independent samples (the research design used in the Algebra I case study) are now available in many behavioral science statistics texts (see Note 15). For the four decision rules given in Table 4.11, these tables indicate a total required sample size of 210 students (with 105 students placed in each group) is needed to ensure a statistical power equal to 0.95.

If the school district's planning committee wished to reduce *only* the two error probabilities used in the Table 4.11 specification to 0.01, the required sample sizes for each of the two groups would be increased from 105 to 194. This would be an excellent sampling decision option. It would provide a statistical power of 0.99, which implies that this new design option would have a 99 percent chance of detecting a true effect size difference of 0.50 (or larger) in the school district population of Algebra I students.

Additional ways to increase statistical power or to reduce required sample sizes for Case Three are given in McNamara (1992c).

Hypothesis Testing Results

The third task in the school improvement case study is used to reevaluate the task force's belief (research hypothesis) regarding the increased effectiveness of the new alternative teaching strategy (Method One).

In this final task, the actual results of the fair-test experiment from Table 4.7 are expressed as an effect size. This analysis is given in Table 4.12. Given a common standard deviation of 10 and a sample mean difference of 12, the actual effect size for the experiment is 1.2.

Using the effect size criterion approach, the task force would recognize that the actual experimental effect size of 1.2 was larger than the decision rule effect size of 0.50. Accordingly, they would recommend that Method One be adopted in all of the district's senior high schools (see Note 16).

All that needs to be communicated to anyone interested in the outcome of the experiment is this straightforward statement: An effect size value of 1.2 tells us that an additional 38 percent of the district's Algebra I students had better achievement test scores when taught by the new teaching method rather than the teaching method used in previous school years (see Note 17).

Table 4.12. Effect size for Case Three experimental results.

Formula
ES = SMD divided by CSD ES = 12 divided by 10 = 1.2
Legend
ES = the effect size estimate SMD = the sample mean differences CSD = the common standard deviation
Interpretation

Given the Algebra I experiment having a 12 point sample mean difference favoring students taught by method one, and a common standard deviation equal to 10 points, the effect size estimate is 1.2. This effect size estimate has the following interpretation:
 	
On average,
    students taught by Method One
        have performance scores
            that are 1.2 standard deviations higher
                than the performance scores
                    for students taught by Method Two.

Case Four: A Nonexperimental Study

The difference between the primary intents encountered in estimation and hypothesis testing studies can be easily recognized by comparing the estimation problem addressed in Case Two to the hypothesis testing problem addressed here for Case Four.

For Case Four, let us assume again that a school district's planning committee is considering a year-round schooling program.

In Case Four, assume that the primary intent of the investigation is the verification of the planning committee's research hypothesis (an educated guess they wish to use in their planning sessions). This research hypothesis is the following: *Secondary school classroom teachers are more likely than elementary school classroom teachers to prefer a year-round schooling program.*

Given this intent, the Case Four questionnaire item for this hypothesis testing study would be identical to the questionnaire item used in both the Case One and Case Two policy preference surveys.

Accordingly, the questionnaire item to be answered by all elementary and secondary school classroom teachers selected to participate in the Case Four study is as follows: *This school district is considering a year-round program. Would you prefer this alternative to our existing ninth-month school year? (Yes or No).*

By contrast, no research hypothesis was advanced in Case Two. What was of primary interest to the school district's planning committee in the Case Two study was the need to estimate three population parameters.

The three parameters of interest in Case Two were $P(T)$, the true proportion of *yes* responses for all 1,000 classroom teachers; $P(E)$, the true proportion of *yes* responses for all 400 elementary school classroom teachers; and $P(S)$, the true proportion of *yes* responses for all 600 secondary school classroom teachers.

These three parameters and their corresponding estimates are also important elements used in testing the research hypothesis (belief) advanced by the school district planning committee.

What should be kept in mind at this point is the idea that the decision rules needed to determine the required sample sizes used in the Case Four hypothesis testing study are *not* the same decision rules used in Table 4.4 to determine the required sample sizes for the Case Two estimation study.

Research Design

The research design used in Case Four is a nonexperimental design. This is true because classroom teachers are not randomly selected from a single population and then randomly assigned to either elementary or secondary schools.

Researchers who use a nonexperimental design to compare two independent groups on a criterion variable of interest (a preference measure in this case) begin their research design planning by first acknowledging the existence of two predetermined groups (two separate teacher populations in this case).

Next, individuals designated to participate in the study are randomly selected from each group and the desired information on the criterion variable of interest is collected from all participants in both samples.

Finally, the data from both samples are analyzed using the appropriate inferential statistics procedure. This basic procedure, which is detailed below, is identical to the procedure used in the Case Three experimental study (see Note 18).

This standard inferential procedure involves the comparison of evidence for the two independent samples. In Case Three, the two independent samples were two groups of students, each of whom were exposed to a single teaching method.

In Case Four, the two independent samples are two groups of teachers, one group randomly selected to represent all 400 elementary school teachers and the other randomly selected to represent all 600 secondary school teachers.

Statistical Inference

Application of the statistical inference model to test the planning committee's research hypothesis is elaborated in Table 4.13. Notice that the five-step procedure in this table is identical to the one used in Case Three.

In step one of Table 4.13, the researcher formulates two statistical hypotheses. The null statistical hypothesis, labeled **H(0)**,

Table 4.13. Hypotheses and decision rules for Case Four.

Step One: Indicate the statistical hypotheses

Null Hypothesis   H(0):   P(E) equals P(S)
Alternative Hypothesis   H(A):   P(E) is *not* equal to P(S)

H(0) is a statistical null hypothesis indicating that the two proportions of yes responses are equal.

H(A) is a statistical alternative hypothesis indicating that the two proportions of yes responses are *not* equal.

P(E) is a parameter indicating the proportion of yes responses for all 400 elementary school classroom teachers in the school district.

P(S) is a parameter indicating the proportion of yes responses for all 600 secondary school classroom teachers in the school district.

Step Two: Specify the decision rules for evaluating H(0)

Reject H(0) if the effect size value observed exceeds 0.50

Retain H(0) if the effect size value observed does *not* exceed 0.50

Step Three: Calculate the test statistic for the study

The essential input information needed to calculate the observed effect size for the two independent samples is as follows:

- Sample proportion for elementary school teachers is 0.41.
- Sample proportion for secondary school teachers is 0.79.
- Sample proportion difference is 0.38.

Inserting this information into the effect formula given in Cohen (1988, page 181), the observed test statistic value for this study is 0.80.

Step Four: Indicate the decision regarding H(0)

The observed effect size value of 0.80 exceeds the decision rule effect size value of 0.50 specified in step two above. Thus, H(0) is rejected and a meaningful significant difference favoring secondary school classroom teachers is detected.

Step Five: Interpret the statistical test findings

The question asked in this policy preference survey was as follows: *This school district is considering a year-round school program. Would you prefer this alternative to our existing nine-month school year$ (Yes or No).*

Given a meaningful significant difference favoring secondary school classroom teachers, the researcher would conclude that secondary school teachers are more likely than elementary school teachers to prefer the year-round school program alternative.

---

equates **P(E)** and **P(S)**. This null hypothesis suggests that the two parameters (population proportions) are equal, implying that any observed differences in the two sample proportions is due only to chance. Thus, the null hypothesis in this model places the two parameters in an equation to infer that the two teacher groups (elementary and secondary school teachers) have the same proportions of their individual members who prefer the year-round school alternative.

Since **H(0)** might not be true, one needs to specify an alternative statistical hypothesis which must be true when **H(0)** is false. Accordingly, step one in Table 4.13 specifies **H(A)**, an alternative statistical hypothesis which fits this logical requirement (see Note 19).

Put another way, either **H(0)** is true and there is no difference in the two population proportions preferring year-round schools, or **H(A)** is true and there is a real difference in these two population proportions. Hence, **H(0)** and **H(A)** are complementary, which means they have no overlap and between them they exhaust all logical outcomes for the study.

Step two in the Table 4.13 procedure requires the researcher to specify a decision rule for rejecting **H(0)**. This statistical decision rule is based on probability and the actual sample sizes in the two independent classroom teacher groups.

With this in mind, it is now time to deal with the sample size issue. Once the two required sample sizes are determined, we will return to this five-step procedure and illustrate how it is used to reach a decision regarding the school district planning committee's research hypothesis.

Sample Sizes

As in the Algebra I experimental study, four specific decision rules must be addressed to determine the two required sample sizes for Case Four. These four decision rules are given in the first four steps of Table 4.14. Each of the five steps in this table is reviewed below.

In step one, alpha was set at 0.05. This error probability acknowledges that the risk of a Type I error is 5 percent.

Table 4.14. Procedures for determining the Case Four sample sizes.

Step One: Specify alpha to minimize the risk of a Type I error.
Decision Rule One: Set alpha at 0.05.

Step Two: Specify beta to minimize the risk of a Type II error.
Decision Rule Two: Set beta at 0.05.

Step Three: Indicate the type of alternative statistical hypothesis.
Decision Rule Three: Declare a nondirectional alternative statistical hypothesis to be used in the hypothesis testing model.

Step Four: Declare the desired effect size criterion.
Decision Rule Four: Set the effect size at 0.50.

Step Five: Select required sample size from sampling table.
Given the four decision rules specified above, the stratified random sampling design used in Case Four would require a total sample size of 208 teachers, with two equal samples of 104 elementary school classroom teachers and 104 secondary school teachers. Since beta is 0.05 in the second decision rule, the statistical power is 0.95.

In step two, beta was also set at 0.05. This error probability acknowledges that the risk of a Type II error is also 5 percent.

Since alpha and beta were both set at 0.05, the researcher is clearly indicating that it is equally important to guard against each type of error.

Note also that setting beta at 0.05 indicates that the desired statistical power for the proposed sampling design is equal to 0.95. Hence, the planning committee has a 95 percent chance of finding a true difference, if it exists, in the two teacher populations in their school district.

In step three, a nondirectional alternative statistical hypothesis was specified. This decision rule specification was also used in step one of Table 4.13 to construct H(A).

Step four in Table 4.14 was used to specify a desired effect size of 0.50. This decision rule which is specified before the required sample sizes are determined provides an operational definition to distinguish between statistically significant differences that are seen as trivial and statistically significant differences that are deemed to be meaningful to the planning committee (see Note 20).

This fourth decision rule is also used in step two of Table 4.14.

It acknowledges that the planning committee is willing to infer that there is a real difference in the preference of the two teacher groups if the difference encountered in the two study samples is equal to or greater than 20 percent.

More important, if the sample difference favors the secondary school classroom teachers, the committee will consider this finding as sufficient evidence to support their original research hypothesis (see Note 21).

Finally, step five in Table 4.14 is used to determine the minimum sample sizes needed to ensure a statistical power equal to 0.95. These minimum sample sizes were located in a published sample size table using all four essential decision rules given in the four previous steps.

The required solution for these decision rule specifications is a total sample size $n(T)$ equal to 208 classroom teachers, with 104 classroom teachers selected randomly from each teacher population. Thus, the required elementary school classroom teacher sample is $n(E)$ equal to 104 teachers and the required secondary school classroom teacher sample is $n(S)$, which also equals 104 teachers (see Note 22).

As in the Case Three illustration, the same general rule holds for this nonexperimental design. *If any one of the four essential decision rules is not specified, the published sample size tables can not be used to determine the required sample sizes.*

Hypothesis Testing Results

Let us assume that the Case Four study is implemented using the two group sample sizes identified above. Accordingly, there would be 104 randomly selected classroom teachers in each group.

Let the sample proportion of elementary school teachers who favor the year-round school alternative be $p(E)$ equal to 0.41. In this situation, the best estimate of $P(E)$, the proportion of all 400 elementary school teachers who prefer year-round schools, is 0.41, which is 41 percent of this classroom teacher population.

Similarly, let the sample proportion of secondary school teachers who favor the year-round school alternative be $p(S)$ equal to

0.79. The best estimate of $P(S)$, the proportion of all 600 secondary school teachers who prefer year-round schools, is 0.79, which is 79 percent of this classroom teacher population. The difference in these two sample proportions is $p(S)$ minus $p(E)$, which equals 0.79 minus 0.41, or 0.38. Hence, the best estimate of the true difference for the two classroom teacher populations is 0.38, which suggests an additional 38 percent of secondary school classroom teachers prefer the year-round school alternative to the existing nine-month schedule.

The effect size estimate corresponding to this sample difference is 0.80 (see Note 23). Using this effect size estimate in step four of Table 4.13, the researcher would reject $H(0)$, the hypothesis of no difference in the two population proportions.

Given these findings, the school district planning committee could continue its planning sessions with confidence in their preplanning belief (research hypothesis) that secondary school classroom teachers are more likely than elementary school classroom teachers to prefer the year-round school program (see Note 24).

The sampling results from Case Four can also be used to estimate $P(T)$, the true proportion of all 1,000 classroom teachers in the district who prefer the year-round program.

This is accomplished by inserting $p(E)$ equal to 0.41 and $p(S)$ equal to 0.79 into the estimation model given in Table 4.6. Recognizing that $S(E)$ and $S(S)$ are not changed, the best estimate of $P(T)$ is $p(T)$ equal to 0.638. Thus, the best estimate from the Case Four findings for the true percent of all 1,000 classroom teachers favoring year-round schools is 63.8 percent (see Note 25).

Resources for Solving Hypothesis Testing Problems

Researchers and administrators in search of a practical guide detailing specific sample size solution techniques for most common hypothesis testing problems can usually find the information they need in basic educational research and behavioral science texts. Unfortunately, such information is almost never found in either a specific chapter or in a single source book. However, an integrated perspective on the four decision criteria used to determine correct sample sizes in hypothesis testing can be obtained quickly using just a few sources.

A single straightforward table detailing specific sample size solutions for most common hypothesis testing situations is given in Kirk (1984, page 475). Similar tables are given in Hinkle, Wiersma and Jurs (1988, page 666) and Shavelson (1988, page 693).

For some, the search for a practical guide may end here. However, let us assume that an examination of a straightforward solution table gives rise to a curiosity about statistical power and effect size, two of the four statistical constructs (decision rules) used in building these informative tables.

Statistical Power

Strategies designed to maximize the ability of a study to detect a true difference when, in fact, a true difference exists in a population of interest (the statistical power issue) are well developed in Shavelson (1988, Chapter 12). His approach is extremely useful for those who have not had advanced training in statistics. It begins by using creative graphical displays to develop an intuitive understanding of the statistical power concept. Next, it links each graphical display to a step-by-step procedure to identify the correct sample sizes to test the research hypothesis under investigation.

Effect Size

An excellent treatment of how the effect size construct can be used to indicate when statistically significant differences reflect practically significant (important or meaningful) results is given in Borg (1988). This text was written for teachers and practitioners who are more likely to be consumers rather than producers of research. However, Borg provides an excellent example of how effect sizes should influence school policy decisions regarding the promotion or retention issue (see Chapter Five).

Borg (1988) also clearly illustrates how practitioners can apply the effect size concept to evaluate published research findings that use experimental, nonexperimental, or action research designs (see Chapters Ten and Eleven).

Theoretical Insights

Three sources are recommended for those who wish to move beyond basic solution techniques and general concepts. A comprehensive guide that provides both the statistical theory and the table construction logic for determining correct sample sizes is given in Cohen (1988).

An excellent graphic overview indicating specific statistical models that can be used to test research hypotheses developed in experimental studies (such as Case Three) or nonexperimental investigations (such as the Case Four comparison of two groups on a criterion of interest) is detailed in Roscoe (1975, Chapter 22). A careful examination of this graphic overview should significantly reduce the time and energy spent on wrestling with sample size and other critical research design issues.

Finally, the theoretical relationship between estimation and hypothesis testing, an essential idea seldom adequately treated in most introductory educational statistics texts, is well developed in Kirk (1984, Chapter 15). This chapter clearly illustrates how the inferential rules for accepting or rejecting statistical hypotheses can be stated in terms of confidence intervals rather than in the traditional form that relies on a designated level of significance and a corresponding critical t test value (see Note 26).

SUMMARY

It is often said that a problem well-defined is half solved. This is clearly the case for the sample size problem.

A sample size problem is well-defined when we are able to specify just two research design decisions. First, we must declare our primary intent to be either estimation or hypothesis testing. These two alternatives reflect the two primary domains of inferential statistics. Second, we must specify the decision rules that will guide our inferences using sample data.

In parameter estimation studies, three basic decision rule values must be specified. These are the confidence value, the precision value and the prestudy estimate of the population parameter. Illustrations indicating how to formulate these specifications were given in Tables 4.2 and 4.4.

In hypothesis testing studies, four basic (but different) decision rule values must be specified. These are the probabilities for Type I and Type II errors, the effect size to be detected, and whether a directional (one-tailed) or a nondirectional (two-tailed) statistical test is to be used. Illustrations indicating how to formulate these specifications were given in Tables 4.11 and 4.14.

Once these specifications are clearly defined, the solution to the sample size problem can be easily determined using published formulas and tables to indicate the required sample sizes.

Specifically, it was suggested that a single formula source from business statistics (Scheaffer, Mendenhall, and Ott, 1990) can be used to determine the correct sample sizes for most common estimation problems, and a single table source from behavioral science statistics (Cohen, 1988) can be used to accomplish the same objective in hypothesis testing. For the record, it is of interest to note that neither of these two practical solution guides is typically referenced or clearly explained in traditional educational research texts.

To bridge the gap between statistical theory and practical applications, several additional sources were recommended. A brief rationale was given to suggest how each of these sources can increase our understanding of the two research design decisions required to solve the sample size problem.

NOTES

Note 1 – Throughout the text references to notes are inserted. The text can be read without reference to these notes. Their purpose is threefold: to extend the information provided on theoretical concepts, to identify a few noteworthy sources on the logic of estimation and hypothesis testing, and to specify a few guidelines for readers who may wish to conduct a school improvement research project.

This is the final chapter of a four-part series dealing with logic of hypothesis testing and estimation in school improvement research. While this chapter can best be understood as a companion to the three earlier chapters, it can be read on its own. However, it would be useful to know the specific topics addressed in the earlier chapters in the series. The first (McNamara, 1992a) focused on the sampling issues encountered in conducting school preference surveys. The second (McNamara, 1992b) focused on effect sizes, and the third (McNamara, 1992c) dealt with statistical power. Both the second and the third chapters were written to examine sampling issues encountered in school improvement research projects that employ fair-test experiments as a means to locate alternative teaching strategies that are likely to be more effective than current practices.

Note 2 – Practically speaking, stratification means creating many lists from a single list. The stratification (or grouping) variable must be selected so that (a) each member of the population can be placed in one and only one group and (b) all members will be placed in a group.

Technically speaking, statisticians say the grouping variable must yield mutually exclusive and exhaustive categories. Mutually exclusive categories satisfy condition (a) above and exhaustive categories satisfy condition (b).

Stratified sampling is used for one or more of these three reasons: (1) to produce a smaller margin of error than would be produced by a simple random sample of the same size, (2) to reduce the cost of data collection, and (3) to obtain estimates of population parameters for subgroups of the total population.

A straightforward overview of stratified random sampling is given in Chapter Five of Schaeffer, Mendenhall and Ott (1990). A review of this chapter should be sufficient for anyone who wishes to design and implement a school preference survey using stratified sampling.

Note 3 – In reporting these survey findings, the actual statement for this 5 percent margin of error should follow the standard reporting formats used in national polls. Modeling the *New York Times*/CBS Poll statement, for example, the margin of error statement would read as follows: In theory, in 19 out of 20 cases, the results based on samples such as this one will differ by no

more than 5 percent from what would have been obtained by interviewing all classroom teachers in the school district.
Technically speaking, there are two estimates of interest in our example. First, the 55 percent *yes* responses is called a *statistic,* which is a summary measure for a set of sample responses. This statistic is a *point estimate* because it provides the best single point to estimate the population *parameter,* a summary measure that can be calculated *only* when the requested information is available for *every* member of the population.

In addition to a *point estimate,* a probability sample provides a second estimate called an *interval estimate.* An *interval estimate* indicates a range rather than a single point. This range is used to acknowledge that the information in a sample reflects sampling error regarding the true value of the parameter.

Thinking in terms of our example, the lower bound of the interval estimate is equal to the point estimate minus 5 percent. This difference is 50 percent. Similarly, the upper bound of the interval estimate is equal to 55 percent plus 5 percent, or 60 percent. Thus, the range of the interval estimate is twice the value of the margin of error. To verify this is true, one can inspect the difference between the upper bound (60 percent) and the lower bound (50 percent). This difference is 10 percent, a value which is exactly twice the 5 percent margin of error.

For the record, it is of interest to note that the *New York Times*/CBS margin of error statement and the sample percent are all that is needed to construct the interval estimate. Moreover, given the theoretical information about 19 out of 20 cases in this statement, one also knows that the interval estimate represents a 95 percent confidence interval.

A less formal but valid margin of error statement is given in Hamilton (1990, Chapter 9). See specifically Hamilton's discussion of formal and informal verbal statements for explaining confidence intervals on pages 261 and 267.

Note 4 – For the record, it is important to remember that every probability sampling design has both a *selection process* (the rules by which the actual sample is selected) and a corresponding *estimation process* (the rules by which the sample estimate of the population parameter and its margin of error are determined). For example, Table 4.1 is a selection process table. Table 4.3 is an estimation process table.

This two-part strategy for probability sampling work is well treated in an easy-to-read basic survey sampling text. See Schaeffer, Mendenhall and Ott (1990). Chapter Four of this source addresses simple random sampling designs, the design used in Case One. For a more mathematical source, deemed by most behavioral science survey sampling statisticians to be one of the very best sources for demographers and social science practitioners, see Kish (1965).

Educators may also want to examine Jaeger (1984) to get some basic insights on how survey sampling can be applied effectively to a wide array of typical problems encountered in educational organizations.

Also, it should be kept in mind that the American Association for Public Opinion Research (AAPOR) has set both ethical guidelines and scientific standards for reporting survey research findings. In addition to reporting the margin of error, there are seven other items that the AAPOR believes must appear in a publication reporting survey results. These are sample size, sponsor, response rate, dates when data were collected, an accurate definition of the population, how respondents were contacted, and the precise wording of questions used in the survey.

An excellent overview of both ethical and scientific consideration to be addressed in conducting and reporting survey findings is given in Chapter 19 of Babbie (1990). See also Chapter 20 of Babbie for an insightful checklist to evaluate all aspects of a published survey.

Note 5 – In this case study, secondary school classroom teachers would be all junior and senior high school teachers. All other classroom teachers are classified as elementary school teachers.

For the record, the preference survey would more than likely include more than one questionnaire item. However, only one item is needed to discuss the required sample size issue.

Also, the preference survey might have included just the one closed-ended question. If this is the case, and a personal interview or telephone survey protocol is used, the interviewer might follow up the yes or no preference response with a second open-ended questionnaire item that asks the respondents to explain why (or why not) they chose the *yes* (or *no*) response.

This open-ended question would provide the district's planning committee with valuable new information to use in the design of the pilot study. Those interested in how open-ended questionnaire data can be analyzed and reported to policymakers and practitioners should examine McNamara, Fetsco, and Barona (1986) and Hanesly, Lupkowski, and McNamara (1987).

Note 6 – Since the primary interest in this chapter is to explain the decision rules used in estimation studies (and to contrast these with decision rules used in hypothesis testing studies), the technical details for determining the three sample size requirements for Case Two are not detailed here.

However, an easy-to-follow procedure for the Case Two problem is given in Chapter Five of Schaeffer, Mendenhall and Ott (1990). For the sample size solution, see page 121 in their text. For the estimation model applied when proportional allocation is specified, see page 117.

Note 7 – The actual selection of the 111 elementary school classroom teachers to participate in the survey would be accomplished by thinking of a simple random sampling design where 111 teachers are to be randomly selected from a total population of 400 teachers. This implementation strategy was explained in the text dealing with Case One.

Similarly, the selection of the 167 secondary school teachers can be accomplished by thinking of a second random sampling design where 167 teachers are to be selected from a population of 600 teachers.

These two simple random samples will yield point estimates for $P(E)$ and $P(S)$. Also, using the simple random sampling design estimation procedures will yield margins of error for both $P(E)$ and $P(S)$.

The simple random sampling design estimation procedures for determining these two margins of error are given in McNamara (1992a) and described in detail in Chapter Four of Schaeffer, Mendenhall and Ott (1990).

Note 8 – The estimation model used to determine the margin of error of 4.5 percent used to construct the second conclusion was discussed in Note 6. Notice that the interval estimate ranging from 54.5 percent to 63.5 percent is equal to twice the value of the margin of error.

Those who wish to use a stratified random sampling design such as the one developed for Case Two should recognize that margins of error for both strata will be larger than the margin of error for P(T).

For example, given the actual survey results where p(E) is 0.35 and p(S) is 0.75, the margin of error for estimating P(E) is 7.6 percent and the margin of error for estimating P(S) is 5.6 percent. Both of these values are clearly larger than the 4.5 percent margin of error for estimating P(T).

Also to be kept in mind is the idea that the margins of error for individual strata do *not* need to be identical values. This is true for the two margins of error above. Specifically, they differ by two percent. Actually, the margin of error for P(E) is larger primarily because the sample size n(E) is smaller than the sample size n(S).

Note 9 – In reality, the school district planning committee would probably also sample both parents and students using some form of stratified random sampling. In this situation, all three survey results (teachers, students, and parents with students in district schools) would be considered in reaching a decision about where to place the pilot test.

Note 10 – The hypothesis testing problem addressed in the Papalewis, Bushman and Brown (1989) study is reviewed in detail in McNamara (1991).

The Hollon and Gemmill (1976) study was referenced here because it provides a summary version of a typical hypothesis testing study addressed in dissertation research in schools of education, especially in departments of educational administration and supervision, educational leadership or educational policy studies.

For the record, both of these studies are typical in another way. Specifically, neither study addressed the statistical power issue in their selection of sample sizes, and neither study used the effect size criterion to distinguish between statistically significant differences that are meaningful (practically significant) and those that are trivial (differences having no real value for making policy decisions).

Note 11 – It is important in statistical inference to make a clear distinction between *research hypotheses* and *statistical hypotheses*. While research hypotheses (see first line in Table 4.7) are theoretical statements and are expressed verbally using concepts, statistical hypotheses (see step one in Table 4.8) are empirical statements and are expressed in terms of parameters.

Note 12 – In practical terms, statistical power is the ability to detect a true difference when, in fact, a true difference exists in the population of interest. Put another way, statistical power is a kind of insurance policy. It guarantees the actual study we propose (including specific sample sizes) is almost certain to detect a true difference if there really is one in the population of interest.

The statistical power issue for Case Three is discussed extensively in McNamara (1992c). A more general discussion of statistical power using the Papalewis, Bushman and Brown (1989) study as an example is given in McNamara (1991). This source provides a step-by-step procedure to determine the statistical power of a study reported in either a journal article or a dissertation.

Clearly, maximizing statistical power (which implies minimizing beta) should be the direction taken in the research design planning phase of any decision-oriented research project. Determining statistical power after the fact can sometimes be a disappointing experience, especially when researchers find out that the actual sampling plan they implemented had only a very small chance of detecting a real difference.

Note 13 – A directional alternative statistical hypothesis that is consistent with the research hypothesis in the Algebra I case study would be $\mu(1)$ is greater than $\mu(2)$. In this case, a statistically significant difference is achieved only when the sample mean difference favors Method One.

Specification of a directional or nondirectional H(A) is required when the traditional t test model is used to test H(0). Specifically, a nondirectional H(A) requires a two-tailed t test to detect statistical significance. A directional H(A) requires a one-tailed test.

Straightforward descriptions of these two testing alternatives in inferential statistics are given in most basic statistics texts such as Shavelson (1988) and Popham and Sirotnik (1992). In practice, a nondirectional H(A) and a two-tailed t test are usually specified. There are two reasons for this convention.

First, a two-tailed test is a more conservative test. This means it is more difficult to detect statistical significance using a two-tailed rather than a one-tailed test. Put another way, if a two-tailed test yields a statistically significant difference, a one-tailed test for the same sample data will always yield a statistically significant difference. However, the reverse is not always true. That is, statistical significance for a one-tailed test does not automatically imply statistical significance for a two-tailed test.

Second, many researchers such as Shavelson (1988) believe a one-tailed statistical test should be applied only when (a) a theory requires a one-tailed test or (b) there is strong empirical evidence (i.e., several prior research studies) suggesting a consistent direction for the difference between two groups.

A specification of the five-step hypothesis testing procedure using traditional t test model for Case Three is given in McNamara (1992b). The reader will see that an effect size rather than t test statistic was used here in Table 8. See specifically step two (effect size decision rule) and step four (actual effect size from the experiment).

Whether the traditional t test procedure or the effect size criterion approach advocated in McNamara (1992b) is used to test the statistical hypothesis of no difference in the two population means, a researcher must still specify in decision rule three which one of the two alternative statistical hypotheses is to be used in the inferential model.

If one wishes to use the traditional t test for two independent samples, the same five steps are used in the hypothesis testing model and the critical t test statistic is introduced as the decision rule in step two.

Guidelines for the use of the hypothesis testing model are given in most basic statistics texts. Two excellent sources on hypothesis testing using the traditional t test for two independent samples are Shavelson (1988, Chapter 13) and Popham and Sirotnik (1992, Chapters 9 and 10).

Note 14 – Wolf (1986) has suggested that an effect size of 0.50 is considered to be a conventional measure of practical significance. Most educational researchers (see Borg, 1988 and Borg and Gall, 1989) agree for two reasons.

First, an effect size of 0.50 will almost always yield a statistically significant difference using a traditional two-tailed t test where the predetermined significance level (alpha) is set at the conventional level of 0.05 and the sample size of each group is at least thirty-five.

Second, uncovering an effect size of 0.50 implies a 19 percent advantage (on the criterion variable of interest) favoring the group having the larger sample mean. A 19 percent advantage is an improvement that is considered to be an extremely meaningful finding in most behavioral science intervention efforts.

It is important to note that selecting a pre-experimental effect size is not based on a hard-and-fast rule. For example, Borg (1988) suggests that an effect size of 0.33 is a good indicator of practical significance in action research projects undertaken by classroom teachers. This effect size implies that a sample mean difference between two groups is one-third of a common standard deviation. The corresponding advantage in this case is 14 percent favoring the group with the higher sample mean.

On this point, the National Institute of Education's Joint Dissemination Review Panel (see Tallmadge, 1977) observed that an effect size of 0.33 or even one as small as 0.25 is often considered to be educationally significant.

Note 15 – The statistical power used for Case Three is given in Cohen (1988, Table 2.4, page 54). This source provides statistical power estimates for all of the most common statistical methods used in behavioral science research.

Abbreviated sample size tables for t test designs having two independent groups can be found in several basic behavioral science statistics texts such as Kirk (1984, p. 475), Shavelson (1988, p. 693) and Hinkle, Wiersma and Jurs (1988, p. 666).

Note 16 – This recommendation is based on the rejection of **H(0)** in step four of the five-step hypothesis testing model elaborated in Table 4.8.

If a traditional t test procedure was used rather than the effect size criterion approach, **H(0)** would also be rejected. Specifically, the t test value for the experimental data given in Table 4.7 (assuming two equal sample sizes of 105 students each) is 8.69. This value exceeds the critical t test value of 1.96 needed to reject H(0) at the 0.05 significance level.

Note 17 – This 38 percent advantage has a straightforward explanation. The Method Two normal curve has a mean of 78 and a standard deviation of 10. For this normal distribution, a score of 90 (the Method One sample mean) has a z score value of 1.2, which is the 88th percentile. Since a score of 78 (the Method Two sample mean) is the 50th percentile in the same normal distribution, the advantage percent favoring Method One is 38 percent.

Also of interest, one can get the same 38 percent advantage by using the Method One normal distribution which has a mean of 90 and a standard deviation of 10. For this normal distribution, a score of 78 (the Method Two sample mean) has a z score value of negative 1.2, which is the 12th percentile in this distribution. Since a score of 90 is the 50th percentile in the same normal distribution, the advantage percent favoring Method One is again 38 percent.

The statistical interpretation given in the lower third of Table 4.12 also has a straightforward interpretation. Here it was stated that the average (or typical) difference of scores for the two groups is 12 points or 1.2 standard deviations.

If 12 points were added to each score for students in the Method Two sample, the new Method Two normal curve would be *identical* to the Method One normal curve.

Also, adding 12 points to each Method Two student score, and then comparing the two sets of experimental scores, would yield an effect size value of zero. An effect size of zero would imply no difference in the two groups.

Note 18 – As in Case Three, the tradition data analysis model is the t test for two independent samples. However, there is a difference in applying this inferential statistics model. In Case Three, one uses the t test to compare two independent sample *means*. In Case Four, the t test is used to compare two independent sample *proportions*.

The t test for two independent sample proportions can be found in most basic behavioral science statistics texts. Two excellent treatments of the two sample test procedures for proportions are given in Hamilton (1990, Chapters 10 and 11) and Hinkle, Wiersma and Jurs (1988, Chapter 13).

In this article, we will continue to use the effect size criterion approach (McNamara, 1992b) rather than the traditional t test strategy. Keep in mind that the same sample information is used in either approach. Moreover, failure to specify an effect size criterion before the study is conducted precludes the use of the sampling size formulas elaborated here for hypothesis testing studies.

Note 19 – Once again a nondirectional H(A) has been specified and a two-tailed statistical test is used. The other option for H(A) would have been a directional alternative statistical hypothesis. While not used here, it would state P(S) is greater than P(E). If a directional H(A) was used, the correct data analysis model would be a one-tailed statistical test.

Note 20 – For a technical discussion of the effect size indicator for testing the difference between two population proportions, see Cohen (1988, Chapter 6).

Note 21 – Keep in mind that the difference in the two teacher population proportions could favor the elementary school classroom teachers. If this occurs, a true rather than trivial population proportion difference is uncovered. However, the planning committee's research hypothesis (belief) would not be supported by the findings.

Note 22 – This solution is given in Cohen (1988, Table 6.4.1, page 205). In statistical sampling theory, the Case Four design would be labeled a stratified random sampling design with an equal allocation strategy.

Accordingly, the reader should observe that the proportional allocation which was best for the estimation problem in Case Two yields unequal group (strata) sample sizes, while the hypothesis testing design in Case Four requires equal sample sizes for the same school district population. This is a subtle difference, and one often overlooked when hypothesis testing and estimation problems are addressed using the same population of interest.

A second subtlety also deserves mention. While these two problems have in common the same population of interest, the required sample sizes to solve these two problems are different.

Specifically, the total required sample size for the Case Two estimation problem is 278. The total required sample size for the Case Four hypothesis testing problem is 208. This difference results because two different sets of decision rules are used to solve these two sample size problems.

Note 23 – The effect size **h** for the test of the equality of proportions from two independent samples is determined in two steps. In step one, the two proportions are given new values using an arcsin transformation, which is described in Cohen (1988, page 181). This nonlinear transformation creates a scale with equal units to detect differences.

In the second step, the difference between these two transformed values is calculated. This difference is the effect size.

This two-step procedure has the following general form. Let **T(1)** be the transformed value of the first sample proportion and let **T(2)** be the transformed value of the second sample proportion. The effect size equation is **h** equals **T(1)** minus **T(2)**.

For Case Four, the transformed value for **p(S)** equal to 0.79 is **T(S)** equal to 2.19. For **p(E)** equal to 0.41, **T(E)** equals 1.39. These transformed values are given in Cohen (1988, Table 6.2.2, page 183). The effect size **h** equals **T(S)** minus **T(E)** which is 0.80.

Note 24 – How confident should this planning committee be given these sample results? This is an excellent question. To answer this question, a researcher can construct a 95 percent confidence interval using the two sample estimates **p(E)** and **p(S)**.

The resulting confidence interval statement is as follows: Given these sample results, we are 95 percent certain that the true difference in the preferences of these two classroom teacher groups for a year-round school program is between 25.5 percent and 50.5 percent favoring the secondary school teachers. Thus, secondary school teachers are more likely to prefer the year-round school alternative.

The margin of error for this confidence interval is 12.5 percent. This difference was calculated using the estimation models provided on pages 411 to 413 in Hamilton (1990). To use this estimation model, sample variances were calculated for both sample proportions. The sample variance for the binomial proportion **p(E)** is (0.41) multiplied by (0.59), which is 0.2419. The corresponding variance for p(S) is (0.79) multiplied by (0.21), which is 0.1659.

Next, both variances were converted to percents and then inserted as sample variances in the estimation model on page 411. The standard error of the difference for these two sample percents was determined to be 6.3 percent.

Finally, the confidence interval estimation model on page 413 was constructed using the standard error of 6.3 percent and a t distribution value of 1.98. Thus, the margin of error is (6.3) multiplied by (1.98), which is 12.5 percent.

An alternative standard error formula based on the counts of *yes* responses rather than the proportions used above is given on page 268 in Hinkle, Wiersma and Jurs (1988). Assuming 43 of the 104 elementary school teachers and 82 of the 104 secondary school teachers have *yes* responses, the standard error of the difference in this estimation model is 0.068 or 6.8 percent.

In this model, the margin of error would be (1.98) multiplied by (6.8), or 13.46 percent, a value slightly larger than the one offered above. This difference (increase) of about one percent will increase the interval estimate by 2 percent.

Note 25 – The Case Four estimate of P(T) is not merely the mean of the two teacher groups, which is 0.60. Rather, the estimate of P(T) is the weighted mean proportion 0.638, which takes into account the differential population sizes for these two classroom teacher groups.

Note 26 – Another excellent source that discusses hypothesis testing in terms of confidence intervals is Hamilton (1990). For a brief but very informative discussion of this topic, see Section 9.9 in this text beginning on page 268.

On the use of confidence intervals to estimate the magnitude of statistically significant differences encountered in hypothesis testing models (such as was done here for Case Four), see the hypothesis testing chapters in Hinkle, Wiesma and Jurs (1988).

REFERENCES

Babbie, E. R. 1990. *Survey Research Methods, 2nd Ed.* Belmont: Wadsworth.

Ball, D. L. and T. L. Schroeder. 1992. "Implementing the Professional Standards for Teaching Mathematics," *Mathematics Teacher,* 85(1):67–72.

Borg, W. A. 1988. *Applying Educational Research: A Practical Guide for Teachers, 2nd Ed.* New York: Longman.

Borg, W. A. and M. Gall. 1989. *Educational Research, 5th Ed.* New York: Longman.

Cohen, J. 1988. *Statistical Power for the Behavioral Sciences, 2nd Ed.* Hillsdale, NJ: Lawrence Erlbaum.

Haensly, P. A., A. E. Lupkowski and J. F. McNamara. 1987. "The Chart Essay: A Strategy for Communicating Research Findings to Policy Makers and Practitioners," *Educational Evaluation and Policy Analysis*, 9(1):63–75.

Hamilton, L. C. 1990. *Modern Data Analysis: A First Course in Applied Statistics.* Pacific Grove, CA: Brooke/Cole.

Hinkle, D. E., W. Wiersma and S. G. Jurs. 1988. *Applied Statistics for the Behavioral Sciences, 2nd Ed.* Boston: Houghton Mifflin.

Hollon, C. J. and G. R. Gemmill. 1976. "A Comparison of Female and Male Professors on Participation in Decision Making, Job-Related Tension, Job Involvement, and Job Satisfaction," *Educational Administration Quarterly*, 12(1):80–93.

Jaeger, R. M. 1984. *Sampling in Education and Social Sciences.* New York: Longman.

Kirk, R. E. 1984. *Elementary Statistics, 2nd Ed.* Englewood Cliffs: Prentice-Hall.

Kish, L. 1965. *Survey Sampling.* New York: Wiley.

Krejcie, R. V. and D. A. Morgan. 1970. "Determining Sample Size for Research Activities," *Educational and Psychological Measurement*, 30(6):607–610.

Kysh, J. 1991. "Implementing the Curriculum and Evaluation Standards: First-Year Algebra," *Mathematics Teacher*, 84(12):715–722.

McNamara, J. F. 1992a. "Sample Sizes for School Preference Surveys," *International Journal of Educational Reform*, 1(1):83–90.

McNamara, J. F. 1992b. "The Effect Size Criterion in School Improvement Research," *International Journal of Educational Reform*, 1(2):191–202.

McNamara, J. F. 1992c. "Statistical Power in School Improvement Research," *International Journal of Educational Reform*, 1(3):313–325.

McNamara, J. F. 1991. "Statistical Power in Educational Research," *National Forum of Applied Educational Research Journal*, 3(2): 23–26.

McNamara, J. F. 1978. "Determining Sample Size in Decision-Oriented Research Studies," *Planning & Changing: A Journal for School Administrators*, 9(2):125–127.

McNamara, J. F., T. G. Fetsco and A. Barona. 1986. "Data-Based Debates: A Strategy for Constructing Classification Systems to Report Questionnaire Data," *Public Administration Quarterly*, 10(3):336–359.

Papalewis, R., J. Bushman and R. Brown. 1989. "District Culture and the School Site," *National Forum of Applied Educational Research Journal*, 2(2):42–47.

Popham, J. W. and K. A. Sirotnik. 1992. *Understanding Statistics in Education.* Itasaca, IL: Peacock.

Roscoe, J. T. 1975. *Fundamental Research Statistics for the Behavioral Sciences*, *2nd Ed.* New York: Holt, Rinehart and Winston.

Schaeffer, R. L., W. Mendenhall and L. Ott. 1990. *Elementary Survey Sampling*, *4th Ed.* Boston: Duxbury Press.

Shavelson, R. J. 1988. *Statistical Reasoning for Behavioral Sciences, 2nd Ed.* Boston: Allyn and Bacon.

Tallmadge, G. K. 1977. *The Joint Dissemination Review Panel Ideabook.* Washington, D.C.: National Institute of Education.

Williams, B. 1978. *A Sampler on Sampling.* New York: Wiley.

Wolf, F. M. 1986. *Meta-Analysis: Quantitative Methods for Research Synthesis.* Beverly Hills: Sage Publications.

CHAPTER 5

Ethical Guidelines in Survey Research

IN their book *Polls and Surveys,* Bradburn and Sudman claim that scientific survey sampling in the United States began on a regular basis in July 1935 when *Fortune* magazine published the first *Fortune Poll* conducted by Elmo Roper and his colleagues. Later in that same year, George Gallup began a syndicated service to thirty-five newspapers that was soon known everywhere as the Gallup Poll.

Today the findings of scientific surveys are used for many purposes. In general, they serve as aids to planning and decision making in government agencies, political organizations, business corporations, and a wide array of not-for-profit institutions.

Bradburn and Sudman (1988) provide numerous specific examples of how scientific surveys are used in strategic planning, policy studies and program evaluation. A few of their specific examples are elaborated here. While no one-to-one correspondence is intended, these examples were chosen with a view toward how scientific surveys can be used effectively in educational reform efforts.

Surveys are often used to help organizations monitor the implementation of specific decisions or new procedures and to evaluate the results of a promising intervention program or a new advertising campaign.

Surveys are commissioned by the federal government to measure the costs of medical care and the utilization of medical services, to evaluate the effectiveness of different types of job-training programs, to assess what is learned in schools, and to measure unemployment rates in different parts of the country.

139

The media uses surveys to measure audience size. These results (such as Nielson ratings) are frequently used to determine the fate of many television programs. The media also uses surveys to monitor the development of public opinion and to chart changes in public opinion over time.

Surveys are used extensively in the legal profession to determine the need for a change of venue and to help lawyers in selecting juries.

Health planners frequently conduct surveys to inform their projections for new programs and facilities required to meet future health needs.

Educational practitioners and policy researchers who wish to use survey research strategies in their reform efforts can easily locate several excellent sources that will help them to design and implement a scientifically sound survey. Moreover, many of the current sources, such as *Survey Research Methods* by Babbie (1990), move well beyond the ideal image of how surveys should be conducted to provide those without prior experience practical guidelines and techniques for conducting real world surveys.

The practical orientation in Babbie's survey research methods book is accomplished in a straightforward way. First, each chapter dealing with a theoretical aspect of conducting a survey also includes an extensive discussion of relevant administrative and practical constraints. This coverage clearly illustrates that implementing the ideal survey research model is not always possible.

Second, case studies of actual surveys are used to demonstrate how the enlightened survey researcher should be aware of these constraints and be able to balance administrative and scientific factors to arrive at the best possible compromise (see Note 1).

The intent of this chapter is to focus on another nonscientific constraint— *the ethical issues* educational practitioners and policy researchers must address when they choose to use survey research as a planning and decision-making strategy.

Since ethical concerns are not part of the scientific method, researchers must look to another set of guidelines. These guidelines are given in the *Code of Professional Ethics and Practices* published by the American Association of Public Opinion Research (AAPOR), an interdisciplinary association of both academic and commercial survey researchers (see Note 2).

In many actual survey research situations, the ethical guidelines directly conflict with scientific procedures, just as administrative constraints sometimes do.

A good example of a conflict between scientific norms and the ethical norms relating to survey research occurs when a researcher uses sample statistics to estimate population parameters.

On the one hand, estimation theory is based on a perfect return rate for a true random sample. On the other hand, ethical norms dictate that participation in a survey must be *voluntary*. Accordingly, following this ethical norm goes directly against a scientific concern that every member of a random sample should participate in the survey.

Fortunately, problems such as the nonresponse bias conflict referenced above can and have been solved by survey research professionals. Along these lines, Babbie (1990) has identified five of the more common ethical problems that are encountered in conducting surveys and polls. Following the approach taken for dealing with administrative constraints, Babbie suggests ethical solutions to these problems that do not seriously endanger the scientific quality of the research.

With this information in hand, the balance of this chapter is devoted to a discussion of each of the five ethical concerns specified in Babbie (1990). Accordingly, the remainder of the chapter is divided into five parts.

Each part is developed in three stages. First, an ethical guideline is given. Next, the conflict between ethical and scientific norms is described. Finally, and most important, ethical solutions to these conflicts are given.

In each instance, these ethical solutions illustrate how professional survey researchers apply methods that do not seriously compromise the scientific quality of a survey. Clearly, these solutions will have direct application in survey research undertaken as part of an educational reform project.

GUIDELINE ONE: VOLUNTARY PARTICIPATION

Survey researchers must ensure that participation in surveys is completely voluntary.

The idea that participation in surveys and polls must be voluntary is in direct conflict with the need to have a perfect (or at least high) completion rate. When high return rates are not achieved, response bias becomes a serious concern.

Ethical Solutions

Overall response rate is one certain indicator for the representativeness of the sample respondents. With this in mind, achieving a high response rate results in less chance of a significant response bias than achieving a low rate (see Note 3).

A quick review of the survey literature will uncover a wide range of appropriate techniques survey researchers have used effectively to increase return rates. An excellent inventory of these techniques, and an evaluation of their potential contributions, is given in Dillman (1978).

Using a strategy called the *Total Design Approach*, Dillman has demonstrated that opportunities to increase the return in a voluntary participation survey exist in all phases of a survey. Several case studies are elaborated in his methods text to illustrate how one can get return rates that exceed ninety percent.

In seeking ethical solutions to the nonresponse bias problem, three specific guidelines deserve mention. First, all potential survey respondents should be made fully aware of the value and justification of the survey. This is usually best accomplished in a letter introducing the study.

Second, the letter (or interviewer protocol) introducing the survey should inform prospective respondents that participation in the study is voluntary.

In some survey situations, respondents may feel that they will personally benefit from cooperating or will be given reprisals for not doing so. To avoid these potential problems, the introductory letter should also provide respondents with clear statements of incentives that can or cannot be expected. In this way, speculation is reduced.

Third, to avoid crossing the line between persuasion and coercion, the survey researcher should seek to find experienced interviewers who are more persuasive than others to do follow-up interviews on sample members who refused the initial request to participate. As mentioned above, this is best accomplished by having a clear statement of the intent and value of the study.

GUIDELINE TWO: NO HARM TO RESPONDENTS

Survey researchers should not harm a participant in any way, whether it is by embarrassment, feeling uncomfortable about the questions asked, or facing aspects about themselves they do not like.

Like voluntary participation, not harming respondents is an easy norm to accept in theory but is often difficult to ensure in practice. While accurate responses are needed to achieve valid survey results, care must be taken to frame questions in a way that will help to avoid possible harm.

In practice, this situation can occur in interviews where respondents feel uncomfortable about reporting deviant behavior or acknowledging low income, lack of formal education and the receipt of welfare payments.

Ethical Solutions

While there is no way to eliminate all possible problems, there are ethical guidelines survey researchers can use to help avoid possible harm. Two explicit guidelines deserve mention.

First, sensitive questions should be asked only when there is scientific justification and answers to them are vital to the study.

Second, sensitivity to such questions is developed only after years of experience and discussions with professional colleagues regarding the appropriateness of specific questionnaire items. Accordingly, the advice of professional colleagues should be used in survey research designs employing sensitive questions, and professional interviewers should be used in situations where respondents are asked to reveal sensitive information.

Harm to respondents can also occur in data analysis and in reporting the results of a study. These situations are discussed in the guidelines on confidentiality and report writing.

GUIDELINE THREE: ANONYMITY
AND CONFIDENTIALITY

Survey researchers have a responsibility to protect the identity of survey participants. If revealing their responses would injure them in any way, adherence to this norm becomes all the more important.

Two techniques—*anonymity* and *confidentiality*—can assist survey researchers in protecting a respondent's identity. In practice, these techniques are often confused. Such confusion clearly limits both the ethical and the scientific integrity of a study.

Put briefly, a survey is considered anonymous when a respondent cannot be identified on the basis of a response. A survey is confidential when a response can be identified with a subject, but the survey researcher promises not to disclose the individual's identity.

To avoid confusion on the part of respondents, it is the survey researcher's responsibility to make it clear to each respondent whether the survey is anonymous or confidential.

In some instances, declaring a survey to be confidential can compromise the scientific quality of a survey. This occurs because confidentiality might reduce the number of volunteer subjects who are willing to participate in the survey. As indicated in the discussion of the first guideline, reducing the number of participants reduces the representativeness of the survey sample.

Ethical Solutions

To help assure anonymity, two specific strategies can be used. If a second mailing is needed to increase the response rate of an anonymous survey, questionnaires are mailed to all respondents asking those who have responded to ignore the second request.

In this case, it is helpful if the letter sent with the second request explains that the questionnaire is being sent to all survey respondents because the anonymous nature of the survey does not allow the researchers to identify those who have already responded.

To assure anonymity in reporting the findings of a survey, the researcher should never report data in such a way that the identification of a respondent can be determined by the reader. Obviously, this guideline holds for both anonymous and confidential surveys.

Here, it should be kept in mind that reporting the results on open-ended questions must be very closely monitored since this type of question is usually more likely than a closed-ended question to reveal a respondent's identity.

When a survey researcher elects to conduct a confidential survey, there are four specific guidelines that help to meet the ethical norms in social scientific research.

First, the survey researcher should be certain that all persons involved in the survey are briefed on their ethical and legal responsibilities regarding the protection of human subjects.

Second, as soon as possible, names and addresses should be removed from the questionnaires and replaced by identification numbers.

Third, the master identification file linking names and identification codes should be known only to the survey researcher. Moreover, using this file to permit corrections of missing or contradictory information should be supervised by the survey researcher.

Fourth, most professional survey researchers are in agreement that all behavioral science surveys should be at least confidential.

Research Design Alternatives

A review of the literature on survey research methods suggests that most surveys are confidential rather than anonymous. This follows because assuring anonymity makes it difficult to keep track of who has or has not returned their questionnaires.

Despite this problem, there are some survey situations where both the commissioning agent and the survey researcher may be advised to undertake an anonymous survey, even though tracking return rates could cause problems.

For example, if a study of student drug use is to be conducted, assuring anonymity might increase the return rate and the accuracy of responses. Also, assuring anonymity allows researchers to avoid the position of being asked by the authorities to provide the names of drug offenders.

If a survey researcher chooses a research design that involves face-to-face interviews, respondents can never be considered anonymous. This follows because the respondent's identity is known to the interviewer.

On the other hand, a research design that involves mailing a questionnaire having no identification number on it is a clear example of anonymity. However, it is important to note here that using hidden identifiers when respondents have been assured anonymity is unacceptable and unethical. In a word, never use the term anonymous to mean confidential.

GUIDELINE FOUR: IDENTIFYING PURPOSE AND SPONSOR

Survey researchers are expected to reveal to all prospective respondents both the purpose of the survey and the actual organization who is sponsoring it.

The responsibility of the survey researcher to identify both the purpose and the sponsor of a survey can sometimes be in conflict with two scientific norms. Specifically, respondents' knowledge of your purpose and sponsor might affect the validity and reliability of answers they provide. In some instances, this respondent knowledge might also affect the likelihood of cooperation.

In practical terms, almost any specification of purpose and sponsor will have some effect on both completion rates and on the answers given by those who volunteer to participate. These limitations clearly affect the conclusions to be drawn from this survey data. However, these consequences are not sufficient grounds for deceiving respondents regarding a survey's intent or sponsor.

Ethical Solutions

Professional survey researchers are in agreement that honesty towards identifying the sponsor of a survey is not only more ethical, but also has a practical value. Dishonesty leaves the researcher open to exposure while the study is being conducted. In a word, the respondent's discovery of deceit may prove to be more harmful to the study due to the negative publicity it may create.

Compared to knowledge of the sponsor, information regarding the purpose of the survey has the greater potential to create respondent bias and is more difficult to disclose completely.

In addition, the survey researcher must recognize that both the actual data and findings of the survey may be made available to policymakers as well as other researchers. Since the survey researcher neither anticipates nor controls how data and findings are likely to be used, the best strategy is to offer a clear specification of the survey's purpose.

With these potential problems in mind, Babbie (1990) suggests that survey researchers can be more liberal regarding a survey's purpose than is the case of declaring sponsorship. Four specific ethical guidelines consistent with the AAPOR code of conduct are advanced.

First, survey researchers should not share specific aims of a survey that are likely to affect the reliability of responses.

Second, survey researchers should share with respondents whatever they can about the purpose of the study whenever this information is not likely to influence responses.

Third, explanations of purpose are better stated in general rather than specific terms.

Finally, survey researchers should never offer fictitious reasons for a survey.

GUIDELINE FIVE: ANALYSIS AND REPORTING

Survey researchers also have an obligation to accurately report both the methods and the results of their surveys to professional colleagues in the scientific community. These reports should include all the problems, shortcomings and negative as well as positive findings of the study.

When I asked my graduate students in the survey research seminar to react to this ethical guideline, I received the following response from one enlightened group. Without any attempt to edit, here it is.

A recent problem with the analysis and reporting of results concerns access to complex statistical packages. With increased accessibility to computerized statistical packages, researchers may include many complicated statistics in a research paper which hide the true results or the fact that the study was poorly done. If readers are intimidated by the appearance of the statistics, they may not be willing to wade through them to discover what the results really are.

Another more personal problem arises in meeting this ethical norm. Specifically, there is sometimes a temptation to save face by describing one's findings as the product of a carefully planned research design, when in fact that was not the case.

Some specifics to clarify the possible shortcomings in a survey deserve mention. For example, a subset of a population of interest might have been overlooked, a response rate for one group might be significantly lower than that encountered in other groups, or a research hypothesis (or question) that seems obvious in retrospect was omitted from the original inventory of research hypotheses (or research questions) used to guide the design of the inquiry.

Ethical Solutions

In all academic fields, science progresses through honesty and openness. Thus, survey researchers can best serve both their academic colleagues and their fellow practitioners in the field by telling the truth about all problems and shortcomings they have experienced.

In many instances, honest declarations can clearly advance a field in two ways. First, such declarations might save others from the same problems. Second, reporting interesting hypotheses uncovered during data analysis can yield productive new hypotheses for future research.

The AAPOR *Code of Professional Ethics and Practices* recommends standard disclosure of a social scientific survey. These standards are elaborated in Table 5.1.

Fortunately, most behavioral sciences provide straightforward and detailed guidelines for describing the technical design

Table 5.1. *Guidelines for publishing survey research findings.*

The American Association for Public Opinion Research recommends that a published survey research report provide an accurate disclosure of these nine research design characteristics.
1. Purpose of the survey
2. Sponsor of the survey
3. Sample sizes used in data analysis
4. Base of response (response rates for sampling plan)
5. Time of interview (dates data were collected)
6. How respondents were contacted (telephone, mail, etc.)
7. Definition of target population (inferential base)
8. Exact wording of questions used in survey
9. Error allowance (margin of error)

features requested in the AAPOR list. However, these technical guidelines are often not adequately treated on the research methods book chapters dealing with ethical and legal constraints (see Note 4).

SUMMARY

The intent of this chapter was to focus on the ethical issues educational practitioners and policy researchers must address when they choose to use survey research as a planning and decision-making strategy.

Following the excellent coverage of ethical considerations detailed in Babbie (1990), five of the more common ethical concerns encountered in conducting social scientific surveys were identified.

In each case, the potential conflicts between ethical and scientific norms were described. Next, ethical solutions that do not endanger the scientific quality of a survey were given. Finally, a notes section was added to recommend a few of the best recent references researchers and practitioners can consult to improve the quality of surveys conducted as an integral part of school improvement research projects.

NOTES

Note 1–In the text, references to notes are inserted. The text can be read without reference to these notes; however, their purpose is to extend the information provided on basic theoretical concepts and to specify a few guidelines for readers who may wish to conduct social scientific surveys as part of their decision making and planning efforts in educational reform projects.

An excellent set of actual case studies illustrating how one can balance administrative and scientific factors to arrive at the best possible compromise is given in Chapter 6 of Babbie (1990).

Those interested in conducting a scientific survey may wish to examine these excellent recent reference sources. On the theory of survey research, one of the most comprehensive and easy to read sources is Babbie (1990). I'd recommend that those who are not experienced survey researchers, but interested in designing and implementing a survey in their own organization, read this text before turning to other sources dealing with specific technical aspects of survey research such as survey sampling designs and the construction of questionnaires.

On survey sampling, a straightforward practical approach is given in Schaeffer, Mendenhall and Ott (1990).

Two practical guides for questionnaire design are Dillman (1978) and Sudman and Bradburn (1982). An excellent source on designing and interpreting public opinion surveys and polls is Bradburn and Sudman (1988). This text is especially helpful in describing what effects polls have on elections, government, business and the media.

For a nontechnical overview of the design and use of surveys in educational research and evaluation studies, see Chapter 11 in Borg and Gall (1989) and Chapter 16 in Krathwohl (1992). On conducting surveys in school improvement research, see McNamara (1992).

Note 2–A reprint of the AAPOR *Code of Professional Ethics and Practices* is given in Chapter 19 of Babbie (1990). Also given in this chapter are seventeen relevant illustrations that identify ethical issues and steps one might take to ensure that the AAPOR ethical norms are met without endangering the scientific quality of the study.

Each of the references in Note 1 addresses the ethics of social scientific research. Specifics are these. For a combined treatment of ethics and legal constraints, see Chapter 25 in Krathwohl (1992). On ethical norms in questionnaire design, see Chapter 1 in Sudman and Bradburn (1982). On ethics and legal constraints in educational research, see Chapter 3 in Borg and Gall (1989).

In addition to these sources, an excellent general treatment of the ethics and politics of social research is given in Chapter 19 of Babbie (1983). Much like the Babbie (1990) text on survey research methods, Babbie (1983) provides a nontechnical introduction to the practice of social research. While it duplicates some of the coverage of survey research, it is far more comprehensive.

Note 3 – At this point, two questions naturally arise. The first question is as follows: *What is an acceptable return rate in a survey?* While there is no easy answer to this question, there are some published guidelines.

Babbie (1990, Chapter 9) suggests that a response rate of 50 percent is *adequate,* a response rate of at least 60 percent is considered *good,* and a response rate of 70 percent or more is *very good.* However, he goes on to say that these are only rough guides that have no statistical basis. To put all this in perspective, Babbie also notes that a demonstrated lack of response bias is far more important than a high response rate.

Similarly, Borg and Gall (1989, Chapter 11) offer this recommendation. If more than 20 percent of the surveys are not returned, it is desirable to check a portion of the nonrespondent group even though this procedure often involves considerable time and effort.

Several practical ways to improve survey response rates are detailed in Dillman (1978). Most of his case studies illustrate ways researchers have been able to get return rates of 90 percent or better.

A good overview of the research on return rates is given in Berdie, Anderson and Niebuhr (1986). This is a very informative reference source on the theory and practice of survey research. It contains an annotated bibliography of over 300 specific sources on survey research methods published over the past 35 years.

The second question frequently asked at this point is as follows: *How productive are follow-up efforts to enhance return rates?*

Put briefly, in many instances, a second or third invitation to participate in a survey can increase significantly the total return rate.

Here is one good rule of thumb. The return rate uncovered in the initial invitation to participate in the survey will also apply for the first two follow-up efforts. This rule can be applied as follows.

Consider a case where the initial return rate was 60 percent. In round two, the return rate would be projected to be 60 percent of the 40 percent of nonrespondents. Accordingly, round two would yield an additional return of 24 percent and the total response rate would increase from 60 to 84 percent.

If a third round were undertaken, the projected return rate would be 60 percent of the remaining 16 percent of the sample who have not yet responded. Accordingly, round three would yield an additional return rate of 9.6 percent.

When these new returns are added to those from rounds one and two, the total return rate would be 93.6 percent.

This straightforward projection can be applied to any initial return rate. For example, if the initial return rate was 20 percent, the total return rate after three rounds would be 48.4 percent. If at least an 80 percent return rate was required for this survey, it would not be productive to conduct a follow-up effort and the survey would be cancelled due to a poor initial response.

On the other hand, consider the case where the initial return rate is 50 percent. The projected return rate for round two would yield an additional 25 percent return. The projected return rate for round three would be another 12.5 percent.

In this case, the total return rate using the three rounds would be 50 percent plus 25 percent plus 12.5 percent which equals 87.5 percent. Clearly, when a survey has an initial return rate of 50 percent, a follow-up effort would be productive.

Note 4 – A wide range of examples that solve this problem are given in Chapter 19 in Babbie (1990).

A good starting point for getting ready to do report writing is Chapter 18 in Babbie (1990). Several additional insights will follow from an examination of Babbie's Chapter 20 guidelines for the informed survey research consumer. Elaborated in a checklist format, these guidelines can also be used to evaluate any published survey of interest.

REFERENCES

Babbie, E. 1990. *Survey Research Methods, 2nd Ed.* Belmont, CA: Wadsworth.

Babbie, E. 1983. *The Practice of Social Research, 3rd Ed.* Belmont, CA: Wadsworth.

Berdie, D. R., J. F. Anderson and M. A. Niebuhr. 1986. *Questionnaires: Design and Use, 2nd Ed.* Metuchen, NJ: Scarecrow Press.

Borg, W. A. and M. Gall. 1989. *Educational Research, 5th Ed.* New York: Longman.

Bradburn, N. M. and S. Sudman. 1988. *Polls and Surveys: Understanding What They Tell Us.* San Francisco: Jossey-Bass.

Dillman, D. A. 1978. *Mail and Telephone Surveys: The Total Design Method.* New York: Wiley.

Krathwohl, D. A. 1992. *Methods of Educational and Social Science Research.* New York: Longman.

McNamara, J. F. 1992. "Sample Size for School Preference Surveys," *International Journal of Educational Reform,* 1(1):83–90.

Schaeffer, R. L., W. Mendenhall and L. Ott. 1990. *Elementary Survey Sampling, 4th Ed.* Boston: Duxbury.

Sudman, S. and N. A. Bradburn. 1982. *Asking Questions: A Practical Guide to Questionnaire Design.* San Francisco: Jossey-Bass.

CHAPTER 6

A Study Guide for Developing Survey Research Skills

FOR the past twelve years, part of my teaching assignment each year has been to conduct an advanced graduate-level seminar dedicated specifically to the theory and practice of survey research. Since the Sociology Department in our university already offered an introductory survey research methods course for beginning graduate students, the original intent of this advanced doctoral-level research seminar was to serve doctoral students in our College of Education who expected to use survey research methods in their dissertations. Accordingly, graduate students in the college who wished to enroll in this seminar were expected to have already completed basic course work in statistical methods, measurement and research design.

Over the first few years that this seminar was offered, the initial student group targeted for enrollment in this research training seminar experienced two changes. First, doctoral students in the College of Education who expected to use survey research in their dissertations were soon joined by others in the college who had a broad interest in learning about all types of behavioral science methods.

Second, graduate students from a variety of doctoral programs on the campus also began to enroll. This group included doctoral students in fields such as architecture, ecology, tourism and leisure sciences, psychology, museum science marketing, public administration, and recreation management.

Consistent with the original plan for the seminar, all students met the prerequisites in basic statistics, measurement, and

155

research design. In addition, several students enrolled in the seminars had previously taken introductory courses in survey research.

In reflection, what accounts for a significant part of the change in the initial group designated to be served by this seminar appears to be the absence of any other advanced behavioral science research seminar on the campus dedicated exclusively to both the theoretical and practical concerns of survey research.

A COMMON INTEREST

Thanks to the diversity of the doctoral students enrolled in the seminar, I have had numerous opportunities to work with both professors and practitioners conducting research studies in a wide variety of professional fields. In most of these collaborative research ventures, my task was to provide technical assistance on the design and implementation of surveys.

On many occasions (which were most likely to arise at the conclusion of a study), I was asked a single question: *Could you give me a reference I might use to update my survey research skills?*

To help me answer their common question, colleagues almost always mentioned that it had been a while since they had taken formal course work in research methods. Moreover, they hoped that the reference I mentioned would include some insights on the state-of-the-art strategies used in survey research.

The intent of this article is to share my response to this question. By extension, the answer to this common question is also identical to the recommendation I would share with educational policy researchers and practitioners who wish to explore how survey research can be used to improve the planning and evaluation of educational reform projects.

TWENTY QUESTIONS

Following the time-honored Pythagorean adage that a problem well defined is half solved, my answer is not a single reference but rather a single list of twenty questions that a researcher must address when designing and implementing an actual survey research project. This list of twenty questions is elaborated in Table 6.1.

Careful inspection of this Table 6.1 elaboration indicates that the list of twenty questions is divided into six parts. Taken collectively, this six-part inventory of questions provides a comprehensive list of theoretical and practical concerns. These concerns range from theoretical issues influencing the intent of the survey (Part One) to practical guidelines one would use to evaluate the scientific quality of a published survey (Part Six).

Three additional features in this inventory of essential questions deserve mention.

First, two questions on ethical guidelines for survey research (Part Two) are included in the inventory to capture both the contemporary concerns and current recommendations of professional societies such as the American Association of Public Opinion Research (AAPOR), an interdisciplinary association of both academic and commercial survey researchers.

Second, several questions are included in the inventory to address the basic concerns that arise in survey sampling (Part Three) and questionnaire design (Part Four). Put briefly, these questions focus on the need for social scientific surveys (a) to use samples that accurately represent the actual population under study and (b) to construct questionnaires that clearly reflect the information needs of those who commission the study.

Third, the state-of-the-art in survey research design now centers on exploring telephone sampling as a viable alternative to the traditional postal survey. Accordingly, the questions in Part Five of the inventory address the wide array of scientific and practical concerns that arise when researchers wish to investigate which of these two alternatives will best meet their specific needs (see Note 1).

A SINGLE REFERENCE

A continuing search of the literature over the past decade suggests that no one publication can adequately address all of the concerns raised in these twenty survey research questions. How-

Table 6.1. Survey research questions for independent study.

This table provides an elaboration of twenty essential questions for independent study in survey research. The elaboration is based on a classification system that divides the list of twenty questions into six parts. Each part focuses on a specific topic. Taken collectively, the twenty questions cover the essential theoretical and practical concerns that a survey researcher must address in conducting a social scientific survey. These questions can be answered using a desk-top reference library that contains six sources. Each of these six sources is identified in the elaboration.

Part One: Theory of Survey Research

Question 1: In his book, *Survey Research Methods*, Babbie (1990, Chapter 1) suggests eight characteristics that make a given scientific inquiry more or less scientific. Describe each of these characteristics. Then use each of these characteristics to illustrate how survey research (one of the many research strategies available to social researchers) fits into the general norms of science and social science.

Question 2: Babbie (1990, Chapter 4) notes that basic survey research designs are either cross-sectional or longitudinal. Moreover, he indicated that there are three basic longitudinal designs: (1) trend studies, (2) cohort studies, and (3) panel studies. Define these basic survey research designs and provide an example for each design.

Question 3: Reasons for conducting surveys are numerous, yet Babbie (1990, Chapter 4) identifies three general objectives that cut across most of those reasons. These objectives are: (1) description, (2) explanation, and (3) exploration. Describe each type of survey and include an example as part of the description.

Question 4: The elaboration model is used to make the relationship between two variables understandable through the simultaneous introduction of additional variables. Describe the logic of the elaboration model. Your description should include an explanation of these terms: (1) independent variable, (2) test variable, (3) dependent variable, (4) partial relationships, (5) replication, (6) specification, (7) explanation, and (8) interpretation (Babbie, 1990, Chapter 15).

Part Two: Ethics of Survey Research

Question 5: Name some of the more common ethical problems that appear in social research and suggest ethical solutions to them that do not seriously endanger the "scientific" quality of the research itself (Babbie, 1990, Chapter 19).

Question 6: The American Association of Public Opinion Research has published both ethical guidelines and scientific criteria for reporting survey research findings. In addition to reporting the margin of error, there are eight other items that the AAPOR believes must appear in any publication reporting survey results. Identify these eight items (see McNamara, 1993).

Table 6.1. (continued).

Part Three: Survey Sampling Design

Question 7: In their book, *Elementary Survey Sampling*, Schaeffer, Mendenhall and Ott (1990, Chapter 3) identify five common terms that are used to describe all basic survey sampling designs. These terms are: (1) element, (2) population, (3) sampling units, (4) frame, and (5) sample. Define each of these terms. Next, use these terms in a hypothetical survey to illustrate how to select a sample from a population.

Question 8: Describe each of the following survey sampling designs: (1) simple random sampling, (2) systematic sampling, (3) stratified sampling, (4) multistage cluster sampling, and (5) multistage cluster sampling with stratification. Provide an example as part of the description of each sampling design (Babbie, 1990, Chapter 5).

Question 9: The American Statistical Association monograph *What Is a Survey?* was written in nontechnical terms to help persons not trained in statistics to better understand both the design of a survey and the concerns to be addressed in evaluating survey results. To evaluate the accuracy of a sample, this monograph suggests that it is convenient to distinguish between sampling and nonsampling errors. Describe these two types of errors (see Ferber, 1990, pp. 17-18).

Question 10: In his book, *Mail and Telephone Surveys: The Total Design Method*, Dillman (1978, Chapter 2) suggests two basic procedures for determining survey research response rates. Describe both procedures. Next, indicate the essential difference between these two procedures. Finally, describe how these procedures might underestimate response rate for mail questionnaires.

Part Four: Questionnaire Design

Question 11: In her book, *Advanced Questionnaire Design*, Labaw (1980, Chapter 2) elaborates several perspectives on what a questionnaire is and is not.

- A questionnaire is a gestalt.
- A questionnaire is not a place to cut the survey budget.
- A questionnaire is not a political football.
- A questionnaire is designed around systematic, theoretical principles.
- A questionnaire is either descriptive or predictive.
- A questionnaire should be accurate rather than precise.

Discuss each of these perspectives.

Table 6.1. (continued).

Question 12: Labaw (1980, Chapter 13) suggests that there are three basic types of questions formulated in questionnaires. Name and describe each type. Discuss the advantages and disadvantages for each of the three types of questions.

Question 13: Labaw (1980) states the following: Unless a questionnaire itself has been constructed with analytic means to distinguish "meaningless" from "meaningful" answers, we cannot analyze the data and know what our results stand for. In Chapters 6 through 10, Labaw elaborates five basic concepts which clarify respondent answers and provide tools for the analysis of these answers. List and describe these five concepts. Then discuss what techniques can be used to incorporate these concepts in questionnaire design (Labaw, Chapters 6–10).

Question 14: Dillman (1978, Chapter 3) classifies survey questions into four categories. Each category reflects a specific type of information that is desired from survey respondents. Name and describe the four categories. Provide a complete sample questionnaire item for each category.

Question 15: The terms index and scale are typically used interchangeably in research literature. Distinguish between these two composite measures of variables (Babbie, 1990, Chapter 8).

Part Five: Telephone Surveys

Question 16: Dillman (1978, Chapter 6) suggests that excellent postal questionnaires do not make very good telephone questionnaires. What are some of the reasons he uses to support this position?

Question 17: Dillman (1978, Chapter 6) elaborates on the advantages and disadvantages of telephone surveys over other survey methods. Describe these advantages and disadvantages.

Question 18: Dillman (1978, Chapter 6) identifies and proposes solutions for several special problems encountered in the design of a telephone questionnaire. Identify these problems and indicate how they can be solved in the design and planning phases of a telephone survey.

Part Six: Evaluation Checklists

Question 19: Develop a checklist of questions that would assist consumers of survey research (as well as those who actually conduct it) to evaluate the significance of a published report of a survey project (Babbie, 1990, Chapter 20).

Question 20: Nonsampling errors can be classified into two groups. These are random types of errors, whose effects approximately cancel out, and biases, which tend to create errors in the same direction and thus cause concern about the conclusions drawn from the survey. Biases can arise from any aspect of the survey operation. *What Is a Survey?* describes ten of the main contributing causes of biases. Identify these ten contributing causes. Next, select a published survey of interest and assess the extent to which each of these ten contributing causes of biases was addressed (see Ferber, 1980, pp. 18–19).

ever, direct answers to each of these questions can be found in a set of six contemporary sources that will provide an excellent desk-top library for independent study (see Note 2).

Each of the six items in this desk-top library is identified in one or more of the questions elaborated in Table 6.1. These items are also identified in Table 6.2, which provides the specific correspondences between these six contemporary sources and the twenty survey research questions (see Note 3).

These two tables can be used as follows. If one wishes to answer

Table 6.2. Survey research questions and sources.

Part One: Theory of Survey Research	
Question 1: Scientific Inquiry	Babbie (1990)
Question 2: Longitudinal Designs	Babbie (1990)
Question 3: Survey Objectives	Babbie (1990)
Question 4: Elaboration Model	Babbie (1990)
Part Two: Ethics of Survey Research	
Question 5: Ethical Guideline	Babbie (1990)
Question 6: Reporting Findings	McNamara (1992)
Part Three: Survey Sampling Design	
Question 7: Sampling Terms	Schaeffer et al. (1990)
Question 8: Sampling Designs	Babbie (1990)
Question 9: Sampling Accuracy	Ferber (1980)
Question 10: Response Rates	Dillman (1978)
Part Four: Questionnaire Design	
Question 11: Questionnaire Objectives	Labaw (1980)
Question 12: Types of Questions	Labaw (1980)
Question 13: Questionnaire Validity	Labaw (1980)
Question 14: Types of Information	Dillman (1978)
Question 15: Index and Scale	Babbie (1990)
Part Five: Telephone Surveys	
Question 16: Telephone Questionnaires	Dillman (1978)
Question 17: Advantages and Disadvantages	Dillman (1978)
Question 18: Special Design Problems	Dillman (1978)
Part Six: Evaluation Checklists	
Question 19: Consumer Checklist	Babbie (1990)
Question 20: Nonsampling Errors	Ferber (1980)

question five in Table 6.2, the primary source for developing this response is Babbie (1990). If one wishes to know exactly what concern is addressed in question five in Table 6.2, this information is given in the corresponding question in Table 6.1.

Inspection of Table 6.1 will also reveal the specific location in Babbie where this information can be obtained. For question five, this is Chapter 19.

With the information from Tables 6.1 and 6.2 at hand, individuals who wish to update their knowledge and skills in survey research can use this desk-top library to assemble a personalized set of twenty responses.

Using this personalized strategy will yield the *single reference* that colleagues so frequently request for independent (self-directed) study. Given this strategy, it should be clear that my response to the question regarding the identification of a single reference for independent study in survey research is not to recommend a single published reference but rather to suggest that each colleague build a "personal" single reference.

INDEPENDENT STUDY

The suggestion to construct a personalized reference appears to have several advantages. For example, responses to specific questions can be developed in any order, and the depth (as well as the form) of the response for each question can be determined by the immediate needs of the individual. Moreover, each of the twenty responses can be updated and expanded at any time in the immediate future.

With this independent study recommendation in place, the balance of the article is devoted to sharing some insights on the concerns addressed in each of the survey research questions. These insights are presented in six separate parts, each part corresponding to one of the six parts used in the Table 6.2 classification system.

It is anticipated that the information provided in each of these parts will help individuals to decide how they wish to design their own independent study plan.

AN INDEPENDENT STUDY DESIGN

My experience with helping both individuals and groups to design their independent study plan suggests that this effort should begin by asking three procedural questions.

The first question is as follows: *Who will be involved in this independent study?* While most individuals initially think only in terms of working alone, this is not the only option.

For example, a group of colleagues who serve on a school district task force that is planning to conduct a large-scale survey may wish to undertake an independent study involving the entire group. Similarly, a group of graduate students and faculty members with a common interest in learning more about survey sampling designs might design their own independent study group (see Note 4).

The second question deals with the scope of the independent study. Put briefly, this question is as follows: *How many of the twenty questions are to be examined in this independent study?* Both individuals and independent study groups will need to address this question. Two examples help to answer the question of scope.

If the school district task force referenced above has six members in their independent study group, they might elect to study all twenty questions. In addition, each member of the group might take the primary responsibility for investigating and reporting the study findings on all questions in one of the six parts of the list detailed in Table 6.2.

A similar strategy could be used by a student and faculty group having a common independent study interest in all four of the survey sampling design questions in Part Three of Table 6.2. If there were four members in this group, each member of the group could take the primary responsibility for a single question.

Consider another alternative. Suppose the independent study group had five rather than four members. In this case, each of four members in the group could investigate a single survey sampling question. The fifth member of this group could be assigned to the task of integrating the group's fact-finding efforts on all four questions.

The final procedural question deals with the sequence of questions to be examined. Put briefly, this question is as follows: *In what order will the independent study questions of interest be examined?* Once again, both individuals and independent study teams will need to address this question.

Consider the case in which an individual wishes to explore all twenty questions and has equal interest in each question. In this situation, a good sequencing recommendation would be to start with the nontechnical questions and then proceed to the more technical ones on survey sampling and questionnaire design.

A good specific sequencing recommendation for this individual, using the six parts in Table 6.2, would be to complete the independent study in these three stages: First, examine the theoretical concerns in Parts One and Two. Next, explore Parts Five and Six. Finally, investigate in detail the specific sampling and questionnaire development techniques addressed in Parts Three and Four.

An independent study group interested in all twenty questions might explore the following two-stage approach. In stage one, all individuals might explore just question nineteen, which deals with an evaluation checklist covering all aspects of an actual survey. Once they share their fact-finding results on this single question, all involved should have a more informed perspective. In stage two, these new perspectives could be used to make more informed individual assignments for examining the remaining nineteen questions. Clearly, an individual could also use this sequencing strategy.

These examples should help readers to recognize two features that directly influence planning independent study ventures. First, while all three procedural questions need to be answered, they do not necessarily need to be answered in the order presented. Getting satisfactory answers on all three questions may involve investigating all three questions simultaneously.

Second, it should be clear that the twenty questions in Table 6.2 are numbered *only* for convenience. Specifically, the numerical system in Table 6.2 was *not* developed either to rank the questions in terms of difficulty, or to rank them in some form that would allow either individuals or study groups to overlook the *scope* and *sequence* concerns raised in the three procedural questions.

To help make a more informed decision on the scope and sequence questions, a brief overview of the survey research concerns raised in each of the six parts of Table 6.2 is given below.

Part One: Theory of Survey Research

The four questions identified in Part One can be used to develop a theoretical framework for understanding science in the practice of survey research. Exploring these questions should help individuals to recognize the need for *focusing* on the norms of scientific activity, *specifying* clear objectives to guide inquiry, and *using* logical methods not only to uncover causal relationships, but also to guard against unwarranted conclusions.

Since my experience in helping colleagues suggests that most individuals are least likely to be familiar with the contemporary literature in this essential domain of survey research, coverage here will be more extensive than that provided for the other five parts of the classification system.

Scientific Inquiry

In *Survey Research Methods,* Babbie (1990) describes science as a distinctive human activity that has eight general characteristics. These characteristics are summarized in Table 6.3. They describe science in general, social science specifically, and

Table 6.3. General characteristics of scientific activity.

• Science is logical *(deals with explanations).*
• Science is deterministic *(identifies antecedent causes).*
• Science is general *(provides probabilistic generalizations).*
• Science is parsimonious *(seeks simplicity).*
• Science is specific *(creates operationalizations).*
• Science is empirically verifiable *(depends on verification).*
• Science is intersubjective *(depends on replication).*
• Science is open to modification *(offers multiple explanations).*

survey research as a method for conducting social science re- search.

A careful study of Babbie (1990) on question one should result in uncovering the following position: Survey research is funda- mentally a rational activity and thus must follow the common sense logic that is inherent to both science in general and social science.

Longitudinal Surveys

It is safe to say that most social scientific surveys are cross- sectional surveys. To describe a survey as cross-sectional means that data are collected at a single point in time from a sample chosen to describe a larger population at that point in time.

In contrast, longitudinal surveys are those that collect and analyze data over time. The important distinction is that changes in attitudes, intentions or behaviors can be reported over time. The three basic types of longitudinal surveys are sum- marized in Table 6.4.

Those interested in using survey research strategies to moni- tor a school district's strategic (long-range) plan or to conduct follow-up studies of former graduates are encouraged to include question two in their independent study effort.

Survey Objectives

While any given survey may purport to satisfy more than one objective, there is generally one primary purpose or objective that dominates the survey. To focus an actual survey, it is impor- tant that the initial survey planning efforts specify this primary intent.

Careful attention to question three will greatly facilitate clarification in this early planning stage. The three primary in- tents used to focus an actual survey are summarized in Table 6.5.

What should be kept in mind here is that much of the recent survey research literature has been devoted to rediscovering the value of exploratory surveys (see Note 5).

Table 6.4. Basic types of longitudinal surveys.

Longitudinal surveys are those that collect and analyze data over time. A longitudinal survey provides a series of "snapshots" that, when pieced together, form a moving picture of the situation and changes that are occurring. In contrast, a cross-sectional survey provides a single "snapshot" of a situation at one point in time. There are three basic types of longitudinal surveys:

Trend Surveys are concerned with a general population that is to be studied over time, but different people will be studied in each survey. For example, we might select a sample of students graduating from High School A in the class of 1993 to determine their career plans. If five years later we select a sample of students graduating from High School A in the class of 1998 to determine their career plans, we are conducting a trend survey. The purpose of this trend survey would be to see how the career plans of students graduating from High School A (the general population) are changing over time.

Cohort Surveys focus on the same specific population each time a sample is drawn. For example, we might select a sample of students graduating from High School A in the class of 1993 to determine their attitudes toward public service. If five years later we select another sample of students from the same class to determine their attitudes toward public service, we have conducted a cohort survey. The purpose of this cohort survey would be to determine how the attitudes of the High School A class of 1993 (the specific population) are changing over time.

Panel Surveys monitor changes over time using the same sample of respondents during each interval. Thus, the "panel" is an established group of people that participate in an ongoing study. For example, we might select a sample of students graduating from High School A in the class of 1993 to determine their attitudes toward work. These panel members (the same sample of respondents) would be asked at periodic intervals (such as every three years) to provide continuing information about work attitudes. Panel surveys are the most sophisticated survey design because they most closely approximate the classical laboratory experiment.

Table 6.5. Purposes of survey research.

While any given survey may purport to satisfy more than one objective, there is generally one primary purpose or objective that dominates the survey.

Descriptive Surveys are concerned with the question of "what is." The survey objective is to discover certain traits and attributes of the total sample in order to make inferences about the total population.

Explanatory Surveys are concerned with "why" something exists, "why" it is preferred or "why" it succeeds. While explanatory surveys provide descriptive information, their primary objective is to make explanatory assertions about the population.

Exploratory Surveys provide a "search device" when investigators are just beginning their inquiry into a particular topic. Exploratory surveys are used to check on preconceptions and to raise new possibilities which can be followed up in more controlled surveys. Exploratory surveys usually take on a more loosely structured format. They often use in-depth interviews and open-ended questions.

Elaboration Model

As a noun, a model is a *representation*. As an adjective, a model reflects an *idealized state*. For example, we often think in terms of a model citizen or a model professor. As a verb, to *model* means *to demonstrate*. Using these constructions, a model as it is used in scientific inquiry can be defined as an idealized representation used to demonstrate essential characteristics of a subject or process of interest.

Thinking along these lines, the elaboration model is an idealized (or theoretical) representation of the process (or logical method) survey researchers use to uncover and study causal relationships.

In its basic form, the elaboration model is used to study the relationship between two variables by introducing a third variable. The result of introducing this new variable into the analysis allows a researcher to determine if a proposed causal explanation for an observed empirical relationship is (a) genuine and generalizable, (b) conditional and holds only for specific subgroups, or (c) spurious and explained by an antecedent variable.

The logic of the elaboration model is summarized in Table 6.6. Items three through six in this table identify the four possible outcomes that can be reached when a proposed causal relationship is studied by introducing a third (control) variable.

Those whose interests center on conducting explanatory studies are strongly encouraged to include this question in the initial stage of their independent study plan (see Note 6).

Part Two: Ethics of Survey Research

The two questions specified in Part Two are used to focus on the ethical issues both practitioners and researchers must address when they choose to use survey research as a planning and decision-making strategy.

Since my previous research column in this journal (McNamara, 1993) provided extensive coverage on these ethical issues, just two points are offered here to guide the design and planning of independent study in this area (see Note 7).

Table 6.6. The elaboration model in survey research.

The elaboration model is a logical method for understanding causal relationships among variables. The logic of elaboration is as follows:

1. We begin by uncovering an *empirical relationship* between two variables which we can call *A* and *B*.

2. We seek to understand the nature of that relationship by introducing a control variable. This process allows us to compare the original relationship between *A* and *B* for all respondents in a study and the *partial relationships* found among subsets of respondents based on the control variable. This procedure yields one of the following four outcomes.

3. If the partial relationships are essentially the same as the original relationship, we conclude that the original relationship has been *replicated*. In this case, the relationship between *A* and *B* is genuine and generalizable.

4. If only one of the partial relationships is essentially the same as (or possibly larger than) the original relationship *and* the other partial relationship is essentially zero, we call the result *specification*. In this case, we have specified the conditions under which *A* causes *B*.

5. If the original relationship disappears in the partials (the partial relationships are all essentially zero) *and* if the control variable is antecedent (prior) to *A* and *B*, we call the result an *explanation*. In this case, we have explained away a spurious (ingenuine) relationship.

6. If the original relationship disappears in the partials (the partial relationships are all essentially zero) *and* if the control variable intervenes chronologically between *A* and *B*, we call the result an *interpretation*. In this case, we have discovered the means by which *A* causes *B*.

Note: This graphic representation of the elaboration model (the fundamental logic used in survey research) is based on the treatment of this topic given in Babbie (1990, Chapter 15). This reference provides an excellent brief history of the development of the elaboration model, clear examples for the four outcomes given in items three through six above, and an excellent set of additional readings to illustrate how this basic logic can be used in theory development and theory testing.

Those who are not familiar with the most recent legal constraints and ethical guidelines in survey research should include these two questions in their study plans. Moreover, if they plan to cover several questions, the two questions on ethical issues should be examined in the initial part of this independent study effort.

Survey Reports

In all professional fields, there is a clear expectation that survey researchers have an obligation to accurately report both the methods and the results of their surveys. These reports should include all the problems, shortcomings, and negative as well as positive findings of the survey.

The AAPOR *Code of Professional Ethics and Practices* recommends that a published survey research report provide an accurate disclosure of nine specific research design characteristics. These are elaborated in Table 6.7.

For the record, not all educational research journal articles and school district reports follow through on sharing accurate information on the complete list of disclosure characteristics detailed in Table 6.7 (see Note 8).

Part Three: Survey Sampling Design

The four questions given in Part Three are used to explore essential concerns to be addressed in survey sampling. These four questions were developed to highlight the use of inferential statistical methods which are designed to make inferences about a population from information contained in a sample.

In many social scientific surveys, technical assistance is secured to design the sampling plan. When this alternative is taken, decisions about the actual sample size and the number of items to be sampled are usually made in planning sessions in-

Table 6.7. Guidelines for publishing survey research findings.

The American Association for Public Opinion Research recommends that a published survey research report provide an accurate disclosure of the following nine research design characteristics.

1. Purpose of the survey
2. Sponsor of the survey
3. Sample sizes used in data analysis
4. Base of response (response rates for sampling plan)
5. Time of interview (dates data were collected)
6. How respondents were contacted (telephone, mail, etc.)
7. Definition of target population (inferential base)
8. Exact wording of questions used in survey
9. Error allowance (margin of error)

volving sampling theorists (consultants) and the practitioners who commissioned the survey.

Sampling Plan

The four questions elaborated in Part Three were constructed to focus on the basic information a practitioner would need to dialogue with a sampling theorist. Accordingly, all four questions can be explored without reference to formal probability sampling and the inferential methods used in estimation theory.

Sampling Operations

My experience in working with colleagues interested in survey sampling suggests that independent study efforts in this area should begin by first exploring just question nine. This option centers on reading *What Is a Survey?* which is a short (25 page) practical monograph covering all the basics of survey operations (see Note 9).

With this information in hand, informed decisions can be made about additional explorations. If an independent study group is formed, I would recommend that responsibility for the remaining questions in Part Three can be explored by just a few individuals in the group (see Note 10).

Part Four: Questionnaire Design

Five specific questions are elaborated in Part Four, which deals with issues and concerns encountered in questionnaire design.

While questionnaires are frequently constructed without technical assistance, this inventory of five questions was specified to focus on the basic information a practitioner would need to work in collaboration with a questionnaire design expert (see Note 11).

Two insights about the coverage of questionnaire design in the desk-top library are given below. Both insights highlight essential issues to be discussed by practitioners and consultants in questionnaire design planning.

Table 6.8. Types of survey questions.

There are three basic types of questions that can be used to design a questionnaire.

Open-Ended Questions. This type of question allows respondents to answer in their own words. Respondents may answer in any manner they wish.

Open-Ended Questions with Precoded Answers. This type of question allows respondents to answer in their own words, and the interviewer then codes these answers into predetermined categories.

Closed Questions. In this type of question, the answers are provided for respondents who are expected to choose the precoded answer which is closest to or best representative of their beliefs, attitudes or knowledge of a situation.

Types of Questions

In *Advanced Questionnaire Design,* Labaw (1980) discusses three types of questions used in a survey. These three types are elaborated in Table 6.8.

While much is written about the advantages and disadvantages of open-ended questions, Labaw (1980) is one of the best practical sources on this topic. Of special interest here is Labaw's distinction between word coding and concept coding systems used to analyze the responses given in open-ended questionnaire items (see Note 12).

Types of Information

In *Mail and Telephone Surveys,* Dillman (1978) suggests that survey questions are used to collect four specific types of information from respondents. These four types are elaborated in Table 6.9.

My experience in working with Dillman (1978) and Labaw (1980) suggests a single recommendation for independent study. Put briefly, a great deal about developing questionnaires can be learned quickly by comparing and contrasting the questionnaire design guidelines in these two excellent sources (see Note 13).

Part Five: Telephone Surveys

The telephone survey is one of the more popular types of survey methods now used in the United States. With almost every household owning a telephone, the access to all corners of society is possible. Also, the availability of random-access dialing increases the possibility of obtaining a true random sample.

The cost of telephone surveys compared to other types of surveying has also made this a preferable method. Both the ability to train telephone interviewers in a single location and the need to use fewer interviewers than are required for conducting personal interviews are two key reasons for the lower costs of telephone surveys.

Several additional advantages of telephone sampling are given in Dillman (1978). These include the following: (1) data can be gathered rapidly by a team of interviewers; (2) direct supervision of data collection is easy to manage; (3) scoring of a telephone survey can occur concurrently with interviewing; (4) the ability to use screening items to skip around the survey is possible; and (5) open-ended questions are more likely to yield higher response rates in telephone interviews than in postal questionnaires.

The three questions in Part Five are introduced into the list of independent study questions to focus on all aspects of the telephone survey alternative.

Those who wish to explore the telephone survey as an alter-

Table 6.9. Types of survey information.

Questionnaire items can be classified as requesting one or more of these four types of information: 1. What people say they want *(Attitudes)* 2. What people think is true *(Beliefs)* 3. What people do *(Behaviors)* 4. What people are *(Attributes)*
Four open-ended questions that illustrate these information types are as follows: 1. What should be done in this school to improve the communication between teachers and parents? *(Attitudes)* 2. In your opinion, what is the biggest barrier to getting students to participate in extracurricular activities? *(Beliefs)* 3. What parent organizations have you joined since moving to this school district? *(Behaviors)* 4. In what school attendance area is your residence located? *(Attributes)*

native to either postal or personal interview surveys should include all three of the telephone survey questions in their independent study plan.

Over the past fifteen years, my experience in using telephone surveys in school district planning and evaluation studies suggests that using just Dillman (1978) provides sufficient information to design and implement a telephone survey (see Note 14).

Part Six: Evaluation Checklists

In professions such as law, medicine, architecture and education, no one expects every practitioner (lawyer, physician, architect or school principal) to regularly conduct research and to publish the results in scholarly journals. Instead, we expect these persons to be current with the scholarship in their fields and to use that information in ways to improve practice. In short, we expect practitioners to be intelligent consumers of research.

With this intent in mind, the two questions in Part Six focus on the informed consumer of survey research. These two questions are entered into the list of independent study questions because they identify two specific sources that provide us with practical guidelines to distinguish between excellent and poor surveys.

Survey Research Checklists

While there are many checklists available to evaluate behavioral science studies, my experience with this literature suggests that the checklist published in Babbie (1990) is the best single source one can use to evaluate social scientific surveys.

The value of this checklist can be easily verified by using its fifty survey research questions to evaluate a published survey of interest (see Note 15).

Nonsampling Errors

To evaluate a published survey, it is helpful to distinguish between sampling errors and nonsampling errors. Sampling errors are errors that result from using responses from a sample rather than responses from all members of a population. In survey reports, a sampling error is expressed as a margin of error.

An example of a sampling error is as follows. Consider a survey designed to estimate the votes that a candidate for a particular office is expected to receive. The results would note that Candidate A's votes were estimated at sixty percent with a margin of error unlikely to be more than three percent. Thus, this candidate's votes are expected to fall in the range between fifty-seven and sixty-three percent (see Note 16).

In a word, all other potential sources of error in surveys are called nonsampling errors. *What Is a Survey?* identifies ten common nonsampling errors that are likely to bias the conclusions drawn from a survey. These causes of bias and a brief explanation of how they are likely to occur are elaborated in Table 6.10.

Obviously each survey is not necessarily subject to all these sources of error. However, it is important to note that an informed consumer of survey research will explore all these possibilities (see Note 17).

SUMMARY

The intent of this chapter was to share some ideas on how either an individual or a group might develop an independent (self-directed) study for updating their skills in survey research. This objective was accomplished by presenting a list of twenty questions (Table 6.1) that a researcher must address when designing and implementing an actual survey research project.

A six-part classification system (Table 6.2) was used to divide these twenty questions into six areas that focus on the major theoretical and practical concerns in the survey research literature. These concerns ranged from theoretical issues influencing the intent of the survey (Part One) to practical guidelines one would use to evaluate the scientific quality of a published survey (Part Six).

A desk-top reference library, containing six key sources, was recommended as a convenient reference system for answering each of these questions. In Table 6.2, a single source in this desk-

Table 6.10. List of nonsampling errors.

Causes of Bias	Explanation
Sampling operations	The sample selection may contain errors, the sampling frame may not include, but rather omit part of the population, or in the case of disproportionate sampling rates, weights may be omitted.
Non-interviews	Generally, information is only obtained for part of the sample. Differences between those interviewed and those not interviewed account for some biases.
Adequacy of respondents	Occasionally, information is obtained by "proxy" respondents. That is, if the respondent cannot be interviewed, someone else provides information about them who is not always well informed about the facts.
Understanding the concepts	Some respondents may not understand what is wanted.
Lack of knowledge	In some cases, respondents don't know the information requested of them or don't try to get the correct information.
Concealment of the truth	Respondents may conceal the truth as a result of fearing or having suspicions about the survey. Socially acceptable answers are often produced by the respondent in an effort to respond or answer in the manner they feel they're "expected" to respond.
Loaded questions	Questions are sometimes worded in such a way as to create a possible influence upon the response to be answered in some specific but not necessarily correct way.
Processing errors	Coding errors, data keeping computer programming errors and such data input methods may sometimes result in bias.
Conceptual problems	Occasionally, differences between what is desired and what is actually covered by the survey allows for errors. An example of such would be using a population other than the one for which information is needed, however time constraints (deadlines) have imposed this alteration.
Interviewer errors	Interviewers may introduce bias by mis-reading questions, twisting (or inferring) answers in their own words.

top library was linked to each question. Whenever possible, the specific chapter or part of this source that addressed the study question was also identified.

Once the questions and their corresponding sources were described, the balance of the chapter was dedicated to providing information that individuals and groups could use to personalize their independent study projects.

NOTES

Note 1 – Throughout the text, references to notes are inserted. The text can be read without reference to these notes. Their purpose is threefold: to extend the information provided on theoretical concepts, to identify a few noteworthy sources that are not included in the desk-top reference library given in Table 6.1, and to specify a few guidelines for readers who plan to conduct a social scientific survey.

The twenty study questions detailed in Table 6.1 emerged over time in my survey research seminar. In each of the past six years, the scope and sequence of these questions as well as their wording has changed to produce the current form of this elaboration. It is likely this inventory of independent study questions will be altered again in the immediate future.

Strictly speaking, these independent study questions are concerns to be addressed in planning and conducting surveys. Since they are not phrased in the form of a question, the reacher might want to call them problems and consider their independent study effort to be a problem-solving activity.

Note 2 – There are many additional excellent sources that speak to the specific concerns raised in each of these twenty questions. In subsequent notes, I will reference a few of these excellent sources.

What should be kept in mind is that the desk-top library sources recommended here were developed (in my survey research seminar) using a single practical decision rule.

Put briefly, this decision rule was to *minimize* the actual set of initial sources one would need to examine while simultaneously striving to *maximize* the coverage these sources provided on each question in the Table 6.1 inventory. Also of direct interest in selecting these six sources were two other considerations.

The first consideration centered on what assumptions should be made about those who would undertake independent (self-directed) study using these questions. On this concern it was decided to assume that the primary target audience should be practitioners and policy researchers who have already completed basic course work in research design, statistics methods and measurement.

The second consideration dealt with assumptions about sources to be included in the desk-top library. Here it was decided that each source in the library should focus (whenever possible) on basic and nontechnical coverage of essential issues and concerns. However, each source to be selected was also expected to have an excellent bibliography for advanced study.

Note 3 – Careful inspection of Table 6.2 shows that the most frequently referenced text for independent study is Babbie (1990). Students consistently choose this basic reference because it moves well beyond the ideal image of how surveys should be conducted to provide those without prior experience practical guidelines and techniques for conducting real world surveys.

This practical orientation is accomplished by introducing case studies of actual surveys. These are used to demonstrate how the enlightened survey researcher should be aware of administrative constraints and be able to balance administrative and scientific concerns to arrive at the best compromise. Several interesting and detailed case studies are given in Babbie (1990, Chapter 6).

Note 4 – On the independent study group alternative, an idea called the Journal Club has a long tradition as an effective training strategy in the natural and physical sciences. In many laboratories, the Journal Club is an activity usually held each week for approximately one hour.

The Journal Club usually focuses on a single article and is organized so that the facilitator of the weekly session rotates. At each meeting, the facilitator offers summary information and provides a critique of the article. Next, those attending the Journal Club ask questions of interest. In this way, the group develops a common language and a theoretical framework for their research.

A good example of the use of the Journal Club in educational administration is detailed in Shapiro and Walters (1992).

Note 5 – On the topic of the exploratory survey, much can be learned quickly by examining the brief but excellent treatment of exploratory field studies given in Kerlinger (1986).

A good overview of the contrast between classical and exploratory strategies in educational research can be found in Tatsuoka (1992). This overview will help to debunk the myth that exploratory studies are strictly "data snooping" and "unscientific" methods.

Note 6 – For the record, all researchers should become familiar with the basic strategy used in the elaboration model. If a theory validation study using an exploratory survey is undertaken, Rosenburg's (1968) classic text on the logic of survey research should be added to the desk-top library. This text provides the theoretical framework used in many advanced multivariate methods such as path analysis and log-linear estimation.

Note 7 – The reader should also keep in mind that McNamara (1993) is one of the six sources recommended for the desk-top library.

Note 8 – My experience with survey reports in education suggests that the margin of error is the most frequent omission, followed by a failure to accurately describe the nonresponse rates and their influence on the conclusions drawn from the survey.

The AAPOR Code of *Professional Ethics and Practices* is reprinted in Chapter 19 of Babbie (1990). Also given in this chapter are seventeen relevant illustrations that identify ethical issues and steps a survey researcher can take to ensure that the AAPOR ethical norms are met without endangering the scientific quality of the study.

Note 9 – Another practical overview of sampling operations, written for those who wish to conduct school preference surveys, is given in McNamara (1992a). Special attention to constructing and interpreting a survey's margin of error is given in this source.

A single copy of *What Is a Survey?* is available free of charge from the American Statistical Association, 1429 Duke Street, Alexandria, Virginia 22314-3402.

I have found this publication to be an excellent document that can be shared with school district trustees and administrators who are conducting surveys. In several school/university collaborative research projects, superintendents have found it very helpful to share this publication with trustees and administrators a week before a proposed survey was presented in their school board meetings.

What Is a Survey? is also available in Spanish. I found this translation to be extremely useful in a recent research training session I conducted in Caracas, Venezuela. More information about this and other available translations can be obtained by contacting the American Statistical Association.

Note 10 – Technical assistance for designing the sampling plans identified in question eight is given in Chapters 4 to 11 in Schaeffer, Mendenhall and Ott (1990), one of the six sources recommended in the desk-top library.

Educational researchers interested in learning more about sampling theory and methods are encouraged to examine O'Shea (1992). An overview of sample size requirements in survey research is given in McNamara (1992b).

Note 11 – Obviously these are the same five questions an individual should explore to acquire these basic questionnaire design skills.

Also to be kept in mind is that both the Labaw (1980) and Dillman (1978) references move well beyond the basic concerns addressed in these five questions. In a word, these are two of the very best practical books available on questionnaire design.

A third source used extensively in schools of education research training programs is Berdie, Anderson and Niebuhr (1986). This is a very informative reference on the theory and practice of survey research. It contains an annotated bibliography of over 300 specific sources on survey research methods published over the past thirty-five years.

Note 12 – Labaw (1980) is clearly an advocate of the concept coding system for the analysis and interpretation of open-ended questions.

A second source that provides basic guidelines for the analysis of open-ended (qualitative) rather than closed-ended (quantitative) responses is Spradley (1979).

Those interested in exploring the development of coding systems in educational research can find several guidelines in Lancy (1993). This reference discusses when and why qualitative is preferred to quantitative research. It also explores a wide range of methods, including those for which the boundaries between qualitative and quantitative research are unclear.

Note 13—While these two experts do not offer conflicting recommendations, several unique perspectives are given in each source.

In examining Dillman (1978, Chapter 3), the reader should be able to identify sixteen basic questions used in questionnaire design. These are formed by combining the four types of information in Table 6.9 with the four types of questions in his classification system.

With this in mind, one obvious comparison is between Labaw's three-part classification in Table 6.8 and the corresponding four-part classification of types of questions given in Dillman.

Two additional questionnaire design sources often added to my desk-top library system are as follows. On questionnaire design and interpretation, see Sudman and Bradburn (1982). For a source that is very helpful to describe what effects polls have on elections, government agencies, business and the media, see Bradburn and Sudman (1988).

Note 14—This includes training school district volunteers to conduct the telephone interviews and working with school district task forces to construct the telephone questionnaire.

Note 15—Most of the questions asked in this checklist can be answered using a basic research methods text. If one wishes to secure an up-to-date basic research text, an excellent introduction to the practice of social research is Babbie (1983).

If the focus of an independent study effort is an educational research project, two excellent basic references dedicated to educational research are Borg and Gall (1989) and Krathwohl (1992).

Note 16—It should be kept in mind that a margin of error can be calculated only when probability sampling is used. On this point and other issues dealing with the margin of error in surveys, see McNamara (1992a).

Note 17 – Williams (1978) suggests that nonsampling errors are actual "goofs" and "blunders" causing inaccurate representation of the population under study.

Schaeffer, Mendenhall and Ott (1990, Chapter 3) believe that the three most likely nonsampling errors are nonresponse, inaccurate response, and selection bias. Several strategies for minimizing these three potential nonsampling errors are detailed in this chapter, along with a checklist to be used in planning a survey.

REFERENCES

Babbie, E. 1983. *The Practice of Social Research, 3rd Ed.* Belmont, CA: Wadsworth.

Babbie, E. 1990. *Survey Research Methods, 2nd Ed.* Belmont, CA: Wadsworth.

Berdie, D. R., J. F. Anderson and M. A. Niebuhr. 1986. *Questionnaires: Design and Use, 2nd Ed.* Metuchen, NJ: Scarecrow Press.

Borg, W. A. and M. Gall. 1989. *Educational Research, 5th Ed.* New York: Longman.

Bradburn, N. M. and S. Sudman. 1988. *Polls and Surveys: Understanding What They Tell Us.* San Francisco: Jossey-Bass.

Dillman, D. A. 1978. *Mail and Telephone Surveys: The Total Design Method.* New York: Wiley.

Ferber, R., ed. 1980. *What Is a Survey?* Alexandria, VA: American Statistical Association.

Kerlinger, F. 1986. *Foundations of Behavioral Research, 3rd Ed.* New York: Holt, Rinehart and Winston.

Krathwohl, D. A. 1992. *Methods of Educational and Social Science Research.* New York: Longman.

Labaw, P. 1980. *Advanced Questionnaire Design, 2nd Ed.* Cambridge, MA: Abt Books.

Lancy, D. F. 1993. *Qualitative Research in Education: An Introduction to the Major Traditions.* New York: Longman.

McNamara, J. F. 1992a. "Sample Size for School Preference Surveys," *International Journal of Educational Reform,* 1(1):83–90.

McNamara, J. F. 1992b. "Research Designs and Sample Size Requirements in School Improvement Research," *International Journal of Educational Reform,* 1(4):433–451.

McNamara, J. F. 1993. "Ethical Guidelines in Survey Research," *International Journal of Educational Reform*, 2(1):96–101.

O'Shea, D. W. 1992. "Survey Design," in *Encyclopedia of Educational Research, 6th Ed.*, M. C. Alkin, ed., New York: MacMillan.

Rosenburg, M. 1968. *The Logic of Survey Research*. New York: Basic Books.

Schaeffer, R. L., W. Mendenhall and L. Ott. 1990. *Elementary Survey Sampling, 4th Ed.* Boston: Duxbury.

Shapiro, J. P. and D. L. Walters. 1992. "Reflective Leadership: Restructuring the Research Curriculum," in *Applications of Reflective Practice*, F. C. Wendel, ed., University Council of Educational Administration, The Pennsylvania State University, University Park, PA 16802-3200.

Spradley, J. P. 1979. *The Ethnographic Interview*. Fort Worth, TX: Harcourt Brace Jovanovich.

Sudman, S. and N. A. Bradburn. 1982. *Asking Questions: A Practical Guide to Questionnaire Design*. San Francisco: Jossey-Bass.

Tatsuoka, M. M. 1992. "Statistical methods," in *Encyclopedia of Educational Research, 6th Ed.*, M. C. Alkin, ed., New York: MacMillan.

Williams, B. 1978. *A Sampler on Sampling*. New York: Wiley.

CHAPTER 7

The Informed Consumer of Survey Research

IN graduate professional education, it is often helpful to distinguish between producers of research and consumers of research. With this distinction in place, professional schools are able to design two different but complementary training programs.

The first of these two programs is designed to train researchers who are expected to make direct contributions to the knowledge base that informs professional practice. Those who enroll in this type of program are expected to learn both the classical and the contemporary research methods that yield verifiable and abstract knowledge.

As producers of research, their careers will be dedicated to extending the knowledge base used in the profession. As this knowledge base continues to change and grow, these researchers will be expected to constantly reaffirm its validity and truth value.

The second program offered in professional schools is designed to train practitioners who are expected to be informed consumers of research. Training in these professional programs is directed toward learning ways to intelligently use the knowledge uncovered by others to improve practice.

It should be obvious that a consumer of research does not necessarily need to know how to produce the knowledge on which the profession is based, but only how to access and use it.

This position can be observed in several established professions. For example, practitioners in professions such as law, medicine, education and architecture are not expected to regularly conduct research and to publish the results in scholarly

185

journals. Instead, we expect these practitioners to be current with the scholarship in their fields and to use this information to form decisions about equity, health care, lifelong learning and the environment (see Note 1).

SURVEY RESEARCH

The distinction between producers and consumers of research can easily be applied to the generation and use of survey research.

Those who conduct survey research are expected to be proficient in all aspects of survey operations. Specifically, they are expected to be skilled in defining research problems, testing research hypotheses, constructing probability sampling plans, developing valid and reliable questionnaires, and applying inferential statistics that use information from samples to make assertions about the characteristics of a population.

On the other hand, no one expects every practitioner to design and implement survey research studies. Instead, we expect practitioners to use survey research information to improve practice. In short, we expect practitioners to be informed consumers of survey research (see Note 2).

There are two common survey research situations where practitioners are likely to assume the role of consumer of research (see Note 3).

First, practitioners may conduct a literature search to uncover survey research studies that can inform either current decisions or strategic planning. For example, educational practitioners and policy analysts might investigate prior research to uncover strategies they can use to improve classroom instruction and the administration of schools.

When practitioners conduct a literature search, finding published survey reports on a problem of interest is only the first step. Since all survey research studies are not of equal quality, the informed consumer of survey research must be able to tell the difference between good studies deserving careful attention and poor studies that are likely to yield incorrect decisions.

In a word, informed consumers of research will need to evaluate the worth of each survey report identified in their literature search.

Second, practitioners may elect to commission survey research studies in their own organizations. In this case, surveys could be used effectively (a) to inform their projections for new programs, (b) to help monitor the implementation of a specific decision or new procedure, or (c) to evaluate the results of a promising intervention program currently operating in their organization (see Note 4).

When survey research studies are commissioned, technical assistance is often secured to design and implement the survey. Accordingly, decisions about the actual sample sizes and the number of items to be sampled are usually made in planning sessions involving sampling theorists (consultants) and the practitioners who commissioned the survey.

Similarly, decisions about specific items to be included in the survey instrument are usually made in planning sessions involving questionnaire design experts (consultants) and practitioners who will use the results to be provided in the survey report.

In conducting organizational surveys, it should be clear that practitioners are not often expected to be either sampling theorists or questionnaire design experts. As informed consumers of survey research, they are expected to know the basic information a practitioner needs to dialogue intelligently with the survey research experts they have commissioned to conduct their organizational survey.

Once the commissioned survey is completed and the survey report is written, the practitioners will need to evaluate the finished product in precisely the same manner they would evaluate the worth of each survey identified in a literature search.

If the survey was of high quality (correctly implemented according to the specifications elaborated in the collaborative planning sessions), it should have direct and immediate application within the organization.

For the record, the final report of a commissioned survey is not usually written in the form of a journal article, but rather in a form that can be understood by policymakers and practitioners who must assume responsibility for implementing the survey findings in their organization.

In light of the distinction between producers and consumers of research, the purpose of this chapter is to focus on the consumer of research. Its specific intent is to provide some guidelines for the informed consumer of survey research.

This objective is accomplished by providing a checklist that practitioners can use to evaluate the worth of a survey report they believe can be used to improve practice. This evaluation checklist is given in Table 7.1.

THE SURVEY RESEARCH EVALUATION CHECKLIST

The evaluation checklist elaborates 100 specific questions that a practitioner can use to determine the quality of a published survey report. In this context, a published survey report can be either an *academic report* (such as a journal article, a monograph or a book) or a *policy report* prepared for a specific organization, a private foundation or a professional association (see Note 5).

Careful inspection of this Table 7.1 elaboration indicates that the list of 100 questions is divided into five parts. Taken collectively, this five-part checklist of questions provides a comprehensive list of theoretical and practical concerns covering all the basics of survey operations. These concerns range from theoretical issues influencing the intent of the survey (Part 1) to practical guidelines one would use to evaluate recommendations concerning the implementation of research findings (Part 5).

Four additional features of this inventory of essential questions deserve mention.

First, twenty-two specific questions on survey research instruments (Part 2) are included in the inventory to capture basic concerns dealing with reliability and validity. These questions were constructed without detailed reference to psychometric terminology. Moreover, many of these evaluation questions are identical to those a practitioner would need to ask when working in collaboration with a questionnaire design expert.

Second, several questions are included in the inventory to address the basic concerns that arise in survey sampling (Part 3). These questions focus on the need for social scientific surveys to use samples that accurately represent the actual population under study.

Table 7.1. Survey research evaluation checklist.

Part 1: Research Design

1. What general topic did the researchers wish to examine?

2. What was the designated purpose of the study?

3. Did the researchers clearly and explicitly state the specific goals to be addressed in the study?

4. Do the goals describe a study that is really worth doing?

5. Was the primary intent of the study one of exploration, description, explanation or a combination of these intents? Does the research design reflect these intents?

6. Did the researchers provide a complete description of the research design?

7. Did the researchers make an effort to become thoroughly acquainted with the literature on the topic of their study?

8. If the study tests hypotheses, does each hypothesis state an expected relationship or an expected difference? Are all hypotheses clear and concise? Are all hypotheses testable?

9. What general (target) population are the findings meant to represent?

10. Did the researcher make an effort to become familiar with the characteristics of the people in the target population?

11. Who was the sponsor of the study? What motivated the study? What provisions were made to guarantee that the sponsor's interest did not compromise either the research design or the study's conclusions?

12. Were the data collected at one point in time from a sample selected to describe some larger population at that time? If the answer is yes, then the study used a cross-sectional research design.

13. If a cross-sectional design was used, did the researchers provide a clear and explicit rationale for any longitudinal assertions entered in their findings? Keep in mind that longitudinal assertions based on cross-sectional data often require researchers to make several assumptions about future directions.

14. Were the data collected at *different* points in time so that the researchers can uncover changes and trends in the population of interest? If the answer is yes, then the study used a longitudinal research design.

15. If longitudinal data were collected, did the researcher use comparable measures and the same questions at each point in time?

16. Were the data collected over time from the same sample of respondents? If the answer is yes, the sample is called a *panel.*

17. If the longitudinal research design used a panel, what percent of the survey respondents provided the required responses for each round of data collection?

18. To what extent does the attrition (responanent dropout) rate for the panel influence the longitudinal assertions made in the study? Was this problem addressed in the study?

19. Did the researchers clearly define their assumptions and the limitations of their study?

189

Table 7.1. Survey research evaluation checklist (continued).

Part 2: Measures

20. What are the names of the concepts under study?

21. What indicators were chosen as measures for these concepts? Do these indicators reflect what has been learned about these concepts in prior research studies?

22. Was each indicator a valid measure of what it is intended to measure?

23. Was each indicator a reliable measure? Was the reliability tested using data from the study respondents?

24. Were indicators (individual item responses) combined to form a composite measure (indexes and scales)? If so, were they appropriate for the study? Were they correctly constructed?

25. Were the composite measures validated to ensure their adequate representation of variables under investigation?

26. Were standardized (published) instruments used to measure variables of interest? If so, were these instruments normed for the target population used in the study? Keep in mind that published reliability and validity information holds only for the normed population.

27. If new survey instruments were developed, was sufficient attention given to pretesting these measures with a sample similar to the potential respondents?

28. If new survey instruments were developed, did the researchers provide sufficient information for the reader to understand the reliability and validity characteristics of these new instruments?

29. If a questionnaire was used, did it deal with a significant topic that respondents will recognize as important enough to warrant spending their time on? Was this significance clearly and carefully stated in the letter that accompanied the questionnaire?

30. Did the questionnaire seek only information that could not be obtained from other sources?

31. Did each item in the questionnaire deal with a single idea and was it worded as simply and clearly as possible?

32. Did each item in the questionnaire include enough information so that the item was meaningful to the respondent?

33. Did the questionnaire use examples that might be confusing or difficult to understand?

34. Did the respondents have the knowledge or information needed to respond to each questionnaire item?

35. If closed-ended questions were asked, were the answer categories provided appropriate for the target population? Were these categories mutually exclusive and exhaustive?

36. If open-ended questions were asked, how were the answers categorized? Did the researchers guard against their own biases during both the construction of categories and coding of open-ended responses?

37. Was some type of incentive used to encourage respondents to complete the questionnaire? If so, did this incentive influence questionnaire responses?

38. If interview data were collected, what provisions were made to ensure that trained interviewers were used?

Table 7.1. Survey research evaluation checklist (continued).

Part 2: Measures (continued)

39. Did interviewers conduct sufficient practice interviews to acquire skills needed to conduct actual interviews with members of the target population? Keep in mind that special populations almost always require unique sensitivities and insights on the part of the interviewers.

40. Were safeguards established in the survey instruments to avoid interviewer bias?

41. Were all measurement procedures clearly and accurately described so that other researchers could replicate (repeat) the study under comparable conditions?

Part 3: Sampling

42. What was the population the researchers wanted to draw conclusions about? This population is called the target population.

43. What sampling frame (list) was used to select the sample of respondents? The sampling frame is called the accessible population.

44. Did the study have good population validity? Keep in mind that good population validity requires the accessible population to be an accurate representation of the target population.

45. Was a probability sampling design used to select the sample of respondents? If not, were any provisions made to avoid bias in selecting the respondents?

46. What specific selection strategies were used in the study? If probability sampling was used, the respondents would have been selected using either a random sampling or a systematic sampling procedure.

47. Was a single list of all members in the population used to create two or more specific population groups? If the answer is yes, a stratified sampling design was employed.

48. If a stratified sampling design was used, were the stratification (grouping) variables relevant for the study? Did each stratification variable have mutually exclusive and exhaustive categories?

49. Did the stratified sampling design yield a true probability sample? Keep in mind that a true probability sample requires random or systematic selection of respondents from each stratum (population group) specified in the actual sampling plan.

50. Was a list of all potential respondents (sampling frame) available to the researcher before the study was conducted? If not, a cluster sampling design was used to identify and select potential respondents.

51. If a cluster sampling design was used, were the clusters (such as schools, families or city blocks) clearly and accurately defined? Were the sample clusters selected randomly or systematically?

52. Was a complete list of the population assembled for each sample cluster selected in the initial stage of the cluster sampling design? Were individual respondents from each sample cluster list selected either randomly or systematically?

Table 7.1. Survey research evaluation checklist (continued).

Part 3: Sampling (continued)

53. Did the cluster sampling design yield a true probability sample? Keep in mind that a true probability sample requires random or systematic selection in all stages of the actual cluster sampling plan.

54. If a nonprobability sampling plan was used in the study, were the actual rules for the selection of respondents specified? Were the respondent characteristics of this nonprobability (convenience) sample clearly and accurately described?

55. How large a sample was selected? Was a rationale provided for all sample sizes used in the study?

56. If the primary intent of the study was to test hypotheses, did the researchers use statistical power specifications to determine the required sample sizes? Put briefly, statistical power is the probability that the sampling design and the corresponding test statistic will detect a true difference if a true difference exists in the population under study.

57. If the primary intent of the study was to estimate parameters (quantitative characteristics of the population) using information from the sample, were predetermined margins of error specified to guide decisions regarding the required sample sizes?

58. How were the sample data collected? Was the data collection method appropriate to the population and the concerns investigated in the study? Did the researchers discuss this issue?

59. When did the data collection take place and how long did it take to collect information from the respondents?

60. How many respondents were initially selected in the sample and how many actually participated in the study? Keep in mind that answers to these questions are needed to determine the actual response and nonresponse rates for the survey.

61. Did the researchers provide complete information on the total response rates and the response rates for individual items in the questionnaire?

62. If a stratified sampling design was used, were the response rates given for each stratum (population group) in the study? Did these response rates vary across strata?

63. If a cluster sampling design was used, were response rates given for each cluster selected in the sampling plan? Did these response rates vary across clusters?

64. Were differences among the return rates for individual strata or sample clusters likely to limit the ability of the total respondent group to accurately represent the target population? Did the researchers address this issue?

65. Did the researchers investigate the extent to which there were any differences between those who responded to the questionnaire and those who did not respond?

66. Were all survey sampling procedures clearly and accurately described so that other researchers could replicate (repeat) the study under comparable conditions?

Table 7.1. Survey research evaluation checklist (continued).

Part 4: Data Analysis

67. What statistical techniques were used in the analysis of data?

68. Were the statistical techniques appropriate to the levels of measurement of the variables involved?

69. Did the researchers select statistical techniques that were correct for the proposed analysis of data?

70. Were the statistical techniques used in analyzing the data applied correctly?

71. Was the percentage of the total sample responding for each item in the questionnaire reported along with the percentage of the total sample who chose each alternative for each question?

72. Did the researcher analyze the survey data one variable at a time instead of analyzing relationships, longitudinal changes, and comparisons between groups?

73. Was appropriate use made of tables and figures? Keep in mind that tables and figures can help to make the meaning of the data clear. They should be carefully designed to present an accurate and undistorted picture.

74. Did the researchers consider how to adjust statistical analyses based on missing data?

75. Did the researchers use the individual as the unit of statistical analysis when it was more appropriate to use group (cluster or stratum) means as the unit?

76. Were tests of statistical significance used in the analysis of data? If so, were they interpreted correctly?

77. Did the researchers overestimate the importance of research

findings that are statistically significant but have no practical significance?

78. Does the data used in the analysis have sufficient statistical power to permit an adequate test of the statistical hypotheses? Keep in mind that all sample data are not necessarily used to test a specific hypothesis. Accordingly, the statistical power for the overall research design may not apply when testing is conducted on subpopulations or specific groups.

79. Did the researchers overlook using nonparametric tests of significance when the data clearly violated the assumptions of parametric statistical tests?

80. If the primary intent of the study was to estimate parameters, were confidence intervals reported along with parameter estimates? Keep in mind that confidence intervals are *interval* rather than *point* estimates and they reflect the actual margin of error due to sampling.

81. Did the researchers uncover new relationships in the data that were not specified in the formal hypotheses or not anticipated prior to conducting the study? If so, was the logic used to uncover these new relationships discussed in the article?

82. Were statistical controls used in the data analysis to study potential cause-and-effect relationships? If so, were those controls meaningful or were they more likely to be unrealistic and artificial?

83. Did the researchers assume correlational findings to be proof of cause-and-effect relationships?

Table 7.1. Survey research evaluation checklist (continued).

Part 4: Data Analysis (continued)

84. Did the researchers fail to anticipate rival hypotheses that would also account for a given set of findings?

85. Were the research findings justified by the data presented and analyzed?

86. Were generalizations confined to the population from which the sample was drawn?

87. Was factual information kept separate from interpretation? This is usually accomplished by using one section for findings and another section for interpretation or discussion.

88. Did the interpretation or discussion section tie together the research findings in relation to theory, review of the literature and the rationale used to specify hypotheses?

89. Did the interpretation or discussion section reference all the problems, shortcomings, and negative as well as positive findings of the study?

90. Do the empirical relationships presented in the report suggest further analyses that the researchers neglected?

91. Could an independent researcher replicate (reproduce) the study findings on the basis of information presented in the report?

Part 5: Research Report

92. Was the research report clearly written?

93. Was the research report logically organized?

94. Were the conclusions of the study presented at a scope and level of generality justified by the evidence provided in the report?

95. Were the conclusions of the study presented in a form that other researchers can understand and subsequently verify?

96. Were appropriate cautions exercised and necessary qualifications made in drawing conclusions?

97. Were all sources referenced in the report included in the bibliography?

98. Did the researchers follow the American Association for Public Opinion Research recommendation that a published survey research report provide an accurate disclosure for nine specific research design characteristics? These characteristics are the following:
   - purpose of the survey
   - sponsor of the survey
   - sample sizes used in data analysis
   - base of response (response rate for sampling plan)
   - time of interview (dates data were collected)
   - how respondents were contacted (telephone, mail, etc.)
   - definition of target population (inferential base)
   - exact wording of questions used in the survey
   - error allowance (margin of error)

99. Did the researchers offer recommendations concerning implementation of the research findings? If so, were these recommendations realistic? Were they based explicitly on findings provided in this study?

100. Did the researchers offer recommendations for future research? If so, do these recommendations hold promise for extending knowledge about the subject or problem area addressed in the study? Do they provide solutions for overcoming research design limitations encountered in this study?

Following the logic used to construct the second part of the checklist, many of the evaluation questions are identical to those a practitioner would need to ask when working with a survey sampling expert to design the sampling plan for a commissioned study.

Third, twenty-five specific questions on data analysis (Part 4) are included in the inventory to address a wide array of concerns about the analysis and interpretation of sample data.

Fourth, the final group of questions (Part 5) focuses on both the ethical issues and scientific quality of a published survey report. A specific question (question 98) is used to address the recommendations of the American Association of Public Opinion Research (AAPOR), an interdisciplinary professional association of academic and commercial survey researchers.

The AAPOR ethical guidelines recommend that a published survey research report provide an accurate disclosure of nine specific study characteristics. These nine characteristics are elaborated in question 98.

GUIDELINES FOR USING THE EVALUATION CHECKLIST

This section of the article provides ten specific guidelines an informed consumer of research should keep in mind when using this checklist to review and evaluate surveys.

Guideline One: Not all questions in the checklist apply to all surveys. For example, some questions in the checklist (such as questions 8 and 56) assume that the survey under review was used to test research hypotheses. If research hypotheses were not tested in the survey, these questions can be omitted.

Guideline Two: Some questions in the checklist ask the reviewer to identify a correct research procedure. For example, question 69 asked the reviewer to determine if the researchers selected the correct statistical techniques for the proposed analysis of data.

Other questions in the checklist ask the reviewer to identify an incorrect research strategy. For example, question 83 asks the reviewer to determine if the researchers incorrectly assumed that correlational findings were proof of cause-and-effect relationships.

In either case, the important point to keep in mind is that a favorable (high quality) response is given for a checklist item only when there is clear evidence that a correct research procedure was used or when there is no indication that an incorrect strategy was applied.

Guideline Three: Some questions in the checklist are designed to be used in pairs. For example, question 47 was used to help the reviewer to determine if stratified sampling was used to construct the sampling plan. If the answer to this question is yes, then question 48 can be used to decide if the correct procedures were used to obtain a true stratified sampling design.

Consider a second example. Question 16 was used to help the reviewer to determine if a panel was used to build the sampling plan used in a longitudinal survey. If the answer to this question is yes, then question 18 can be used to decide if the attrition (respondent dropout) rate for the panel influenced the longitudinal assertions made in the study.

The important point is that when a pair of checklist questions are appropriate for the review of a particular survey, only one favorable or unfavorable response needs to be recorded for the evaluation decision on this pair of questions. In the two examples given above, favorable (high quality) or unfavorable (low quality) responses will depend on the answers to question 18 and question 48.

Guideline Four: The logic used to construct the evaluation checklist requires a qualitative rather than a quantitative response for each checklist question. To be more specific, the checklist was *not* designed so that reviewers can give quantitative ratings to individual items and then sum these individual values to produce a single overall quantitative rating for a survey.

The intent of this evaluation checklist was to determine the overall quality of a survey by asking the reviewer to complete three specific tasks.

In step one, the reviewer should identify favorable (high quality) or unfavorable (low quality) responses (informed judgments) for each appropriate question in the checklist.

In step two, the reviewer should continue the evaluation by examining all the responses (informed judgments) recorded for

Part 1 of the checklist. This evaluation should produce a favorable or unfavorable position on the quality of the survey research operations involved in the research design.

This procedure should be repeated for each of the four remaining parts of the checklist. Each time the reviewer should determine if the survey being reviewed should receive a favorable (high) or unfavorable (low) evaluation on that aspect of survey operations.

In the final step, the reviewer should analyze the five aggregate judgments (informed responses) given for each of the five parts of the checklist. These five aggregate judgments represented the outcomes from implementing step two.

Obviously, a favorable overall response for each of the five parts of the checklist would clearly suggest that the survey being reviewed was of high quality. Accordingly, consumers of research can use the survey results from this study without reservations to inform decisions in their own practicing professional environment.

On the other hand, if the third step of the review yielded unfavorable responses for one or more of the five parts in the checklist, it is certain that the quality of the survey under review is in question. If serious questions can be raised about the scientific quality of a survey, informed consumers of research would be wise to discard the study and set aside any ideas about using the findings of this survey to inform practice.

It is important to recognize here that it is often hard for school practitioners (and educational researchers as well) to discard or set aside the findings from low quality studies, especially when these studies appear to support their beliefs about how to improve teaching and learning in schools.

Guideline Five: The reviewer can use basic research texts to secure answers for almost all questions in the checklist. This is true because questions in the checklist deal primarily with the logic of survey research rather than with technical details experts must employ (see Note 6).

If reviewers encounter relevant checklist questions they are unable to answer, there is no need to panic. In this situation, it is wise to reference the time-honored Pythagorean adage that a problem well-defined is half solved. The solution to the problem at hand can often be determined either by consulting the appropriate section of a basic research text or by sharing this well-defined problem with an appropriate survey research expert.

Guideline Six: If a survey instrument has poor reliability and validity, these are sufficient grounds for the reviewer to give the survey an overall unfavorable (low quality) rating. In a word, if a survey instrument does not measure what a researcher intends it to measure, using excellent data analysis procedures will not remedy this problem.

Guideline Seven: If a sampling plan is poorly designed or if it is not correctly executed, this is sufficient grounds for the reviewer to give the survey an overall unfavorable (low quality) rating. In a word, if the sampling plan does not produce a representative sample, neither a valid questionnaire nor an excellent data analysis strategy will yield findings that accurately represent the population under study.

Guideline Eight: If a survey reports statistically significant results, the reviewer will need to determine if these statistically significant results reflect trivial or meaningful differences. In this case, two different situations are possible.

If the researchers discuss the difference between statistically significant and meaningful (practically significant) differences, this discussion should provide sufficient evidence to evaluate their findings.

If the researchers report only statistically significant results, the reviewer may still be able to determine if these results are meaningful. Guidelines for making these decisions are given in most research methods texts (see Note 7).

Guideline Nine: If the survey tests research hypotheses, the reviewer should look for the statistical power corresponding to each research hypothesis tested. If statistical power entries are not given in the published report, these values can be determined in a straightforward way (see Note 8).

The point to keep in mind here is that statistical power (the ability to detect a true difference in the population of interest) will almost always differ for different research designs, and in some cases, for different statistical tests reported in the same study.

High statistical power (high ability to detect a true difference) should be rewarded with favorable (high quality) ratings. On the other hand, low statistical power is usually sufficient evidence for a reviewer to discard a study. This follows because low statistical power implies that a study has a very low probability of detecting a real difference in the population under study. This is especially true when researchers place high confidence in low corresponding significance levels.

Guideline Ten: If a study provides statistical estimates for population values, the reviewer should look for the margin of error corresponding to each estimate. If a margin of error is given for a population estimate, this should be taken into account in evaluating the accuracy of the estimate. If a margin of error is not reported for a population estimate, the margin of error can often be determined using the sample data published in the report (see Note 9).

The important idea here is that every estimate of a population value (called a parameter) derived from information found in a probability sample will have a margin of error. If the margin of error is large, or if the margin of error cannot be determined, this is usually sufficient grounds to set aside the findings (see Note 10).

IMPLICATIONS

These ten guidelines were not written with the idea that collectively they would address everything an informed consumer would need to know about how to evaluate survey research. However, it was anticipated that learning to answer the 100 questions in this survey research evaluation checklist would reveal other specific recommendations that practitioners will want to use as they become informed consumers of research.

While most practitioners usually think only in terms of working alone to evaluate individual studies, this is not the only option. Professional colleagues who share a common interest in using research findings to inform practice can easily form a study group to investigate the research literature on a topic of interest.

On the independent study group alternative, an idea called the

Journal Club has a long tradition as an effective learning strategy in the natural and physical sciences. In many laboratories, the Journal Club is an activity usually held each week for approximately one hour.

The Journal Club usually focuses on a single article and is organized so that the facilitator of the weekly session rotates. At each meeting, the facilitator offers summary information and provides a critique of the article. In this way, the group develops a common language and a theoretical framework for evaluating relevant research. A good example of the use of the Journal Club in school administration is detailed in Shapiro and Walters (1992).

NOTES

Note 1 – Throughout the text, references to notes are inserted. The text can be read without reference to these notes. Their purpose is to extend the information provided in the article and to identify a few noteworthy sources for readers who plan to use the survey research evaluation checklist.

My explanation of the distinction between producers and consumers of research was directly influenced by the application of this distinction in the design of the NOVA University research training program for practicing school administrators given in Haller (1992).

Note 2 – My use of the distinction between producers and consumers of survey research has evolved over the past ten years in my advanced doctoral seminar on survey research methods taught at Texas A&M University.

For the record, the use of this distinction in the field of educational administration was advanced over thirty years ago by Andrews (1963). The suggestions given by Andrews were sound. They still hold today and are reflected in this article. Those responsible for the graduate research training of school practitioners would do well to revisit the suggestions offered in this 1963 reference.

Note 3 – The two ways that I have suggested for how practitioners can be consumers of survey research correspond directly to the two types of educational research identified in *Research for Tomorrow's Schools,* a report published by the National Academy of Education in 1969. This landmark report (see Cronbach and Suppes, 1969) shares conclusions on how the education professions could make more effective use of research and scholarship to improve classroom instruction and the administration of schools.

To be more specific, conducting literature searches corresponds to using research findings from *conclusion-oriented inquiries,* and commissioning organizational surveys corresponds to using research findings from *decision-oriented inquiries.*

A brief discussion of these two types of inquiry is given in McNamara (1992c). On the two ways school practitioners can use research, see also Kowalski and Reitzug (1993, Chapter 3).

Note 4 – Each of these three opportunities for practitioners to use survey research findings in their own organizations has a formal name in the evaluation literature. Corresponding names are as follows: (a) needs assessment, (b) formative evaluation, and (c) summative evaluation.

A description of these terms and their implications for evaluation in specific organizational settings is given in Isaac and Michael (1981).

Note 5 – I first encountered the idea of thinking in terms of "the informed consumer of survey research" over fifteen years ago in Earl Babbie's excellent first edition of *Survey Research Methods.* This perspective has been enlarged and is available in Chapter 20 in the new edition of Babbie (1990).

Construction of the 100 evaluation questions elaborated in the Table 7.1 checklist was informed by checklists and research evaluation guidelines encountered in several behavioral science and educational research methods texts.

In addition to Babbie (1990, Chapter 20), helpful suggestions were found in Berdie, Anderson and Niebuhr (1986), Best and Kahn (1993), Borg and Gall (1989), Fraenkel and Wallen (1993), Isaac and Michael (1981), Krathwohl (1992), Lancy (1993), O'Shea (1992) and Spradley (1979). Each of these sources provides basic information and clear insights one can use to answer questions elaborated in the Table 7.1 checklist.

Note 6 – For the record, my two prior research columns in

Volume Two of the *IJER* were both written to explore the use of survey research methods in school improvement research. Ethical guidelines for survey research were discussed in McNamara (1993a). Developing an independent study program to update skills in all aspects of survey operations was discussed in McNamara (1993b).

The independent study guide given in McNamara (1993b) is based on using six basic references that practitioners can use to answer almost all 100 questions raised in the Table 7.1 checklist. Since this article identifies specific chapters or sections to be read in each of these six sources, I'd recommend that these six sources be consulted before one elects to explore other references.

The six sources to be used with the study guide are Babbie (1990), Dillman (1978), Ferber (1980), Labaw (1980), McNamara (1993a), and Schaeffer, Mendenhall and Ott (1990).

Those whose interest centers on the use of survey research findings to inform decisions are also encouraged to examine Bradburn and Sudman (1988). On questionnaire design, see Sudman and Bradburn (1982). On designing and implementing policy preference surveys in the schools, see McNamara (1992a).

If one wishes to get a clear but nontechnical overview of the logic of survey research, an excellent classic work on this topic is Rosenburg (1968). This basic source is still widely referenced for the development of state-of-the-art multivariate statistical methods and research procedures.

Note 7 – A straightforward method for distinguishing between statistically significant findings that are meaningful (practically significant) and those that are trivial is given in McNamara (1992b).

This method uses only the published sample information given on means, standard deviations and the actual sample sizes. Such information is usually given in the data analysis section of the published article. It is precisely the same information researchers use to determine test statistics to evaluate statistical hypotheses.

Note 8 – Guidelines for determining the statistical power of a published research article are given in McNamara (1991).

On using statistical power concepts to design practical research studies that have an excellent chance to detect true differences in the population of interest, see McNamara (1992c). On the differences between survey studies directed toward either hypothesis testing or estimation, see McNamara (1992d).

Note 9 – Basic guidelines for calculating and interpreting margins of error are provided in McNamara (1992a). A comprehensive treatment of margins of error for most behavioral science surveys is given in Schaeffer, Mendenhall and Ott (1990).

Note 10 – Recall that the AAPOR ethical guidelines for reporting survey research findings require researchers to provide a margin of error for each parameter estimate. On this point, see question 98 in the Table 7.1 checklist.

It should be of some interest to note that very few educational research journal articles and school district reports follow through on the margin of error disclosure recommendation given in the AAPOR *Code of Professional Ethics and Practices.*

This shortcoming is probably due to the fact that educational research method texts almost never reference the AAPOR Code in their treatment of survey research. This code is printed in Chapter 19 of Babbie (1990). Also included in this chapter of Babbie are several relevant illustrations on how this code can be applied in real world research situations.

REFERENCES

Andrews, J. H. 1963. "Differentiated Research Training for Students of Administration," in *Eductional Research: New Perspectives,* J. A. Culbertson and S. P. Hencley, eds., Danville, IL: Interstate Publishers & Printers.

Babbie, E. 1990. *Survey Research Methods, 2nd Ed.* Belmont, CA: Wadsworth.

Berdie, D. R., J. F. Anderson and M. A. Niebuhr. 1986. *Questionnaires: Design and Use, 2nd Ed.* Metuchen, NJ: Scarecrow Press.

Best, J. W. and J. V. Kahn. 1993. *Research in Education, 7th Ed.* Boston: Allyn and Bacon.

Borg, W. A. and M. Gall. 1989. *Educational Research, 5th Ed.* New York: Longman.

Bradburn, N. M. and S. Sudman. 1988. *Polls and Surveys: Understanding What They Tell Us.* San Francisco: Jossey-Bass.

Cronbach, L. J. and P. Suppes, eds. 1969. *Research for Tomorrow's Schools: Disciplined Inquiry for Education.* New York: MacMillan.

Dillman, D. A. 1978. *Mail and Telephone Surveys: The Total Design Method.* New York: Wiley.

Ferber, R., ed. 1980. *What Is a Survey?* Alexandria, VA: American Statistical Association.

Fraenkel, J. R. and N. E. Wallen. 1993. *How to Design and Evaluate Research in Education, 2nd Ed.* New York: McGraw-Hill.

Haller, E. J. 1992. *Study Guide for Research for School Improvement: Academic Year 1992–93.* National Ed.D. Program for Educational Leaders, Nova University, Fort Lauderdale, FL 33314.

Isaac, S. and W. B. Michael. 1981. *Handbook in Research and Evaluation for Education and the Behavioral Sciences, 2nd Ed.* San Diego: EDITS Publishers.

Kowalski, T. J. and U. C. Reitzug. 1993. *Contemporary School Administration.* New York: Longman.

Krathwohl, D. A. 1992. *Methods of Educational and Social Science Research.* New York: Longman.

Labaw, P. 1980. *Advanced Questionnaire Design, 2nd Ed.* Cambridge, MA: Abt Books.

Lancy, D. F. 1993. *Qualitative Research in Education: An Introduction to the Major Traditions.* New York: Longman.

McNamara, J. F. 1993a. "Ethical Guidelines in Survey Research," *International Journal of Educational Reform,* 2(1):96–101.

McNamara, J. F. 1993b. "A Study Guide for Developing Survey Research Skills," *International Journal of Educational Reform,* 2(2):213–223.

McNamara, J. F. 1992a. "Sample Size for School Preference Surveys," *International Journal of Educational Reform,* 1(1):83–90.

McNamara, J. F. 1992b. "The Effect Size Criterion in School Improvement Research," *International Journal of Educational Reform,* 1(2):191–202.

McNamara, J. F. 1992c. "Statistical Power in School Improvement Research," *International Journal of Educational Reform,* 1(3):313–325.

McNamara, J. F. 1992d. "Research Designs and Sample Size Requirements in School Improvement Research," *International Journal of Educational Reform,* 1(4):433–451.

McNamara, J. F. 1991. "Statistical Power in Educational Research," *National Forum of Applied Educational Research Journal,* 3(2):23–36.

O'Shea, D. W. 1992. "Survey Design," in *Encyclopedia of Educational Research, 6th Ed.* M. C. Alkin, ed., New York: MacMillan.

Rosenburg, M. 1968. *The Logic of Survey Research.* New York: Basic Books.

Schaeffer, R. L., W. Mendenhall and L. Ott. 1990. *Elementary Survey Sampling, 4th Ed.* Boston: Duxbury.

Shapiro, J. P. and D. L. Walter. 1992. "Reflective Leadership: Restructuring the Research Curriculum," in *Applications of Reflective Practice,* F. C. Wendel, ed., University Council of Educational Administration, The Pennsylvania State University, University Park, PA 16802-3200.

Spradley, J. P. 1979. *The Ethnographic Interview.* Fort Worth, TX: Harcourt Brace Jovanovich.

Sudman, S. and N. A. Bradburn. 1982. *Asking Questions: A Practical Guide to Questionnaire Design.* San Francisco: Jossey-Bass.

Table A. Sample size for Problem 1.1.

Initial Calculations	
Step One:	$NPQ = (800) (0.50) (0.50) = 200$
Step Two:	$C = (0.05) (0.05) = 0.0025$
Step Three:	$D = C/A = 0.0025/3.84 = 0.000651$
Step Four:	$(N-1)D = (800-1) (0.000651) = 0.5202$
Step Five:	$PQ = (0.50) (0.50) = 0.25$

Recommended Sample Size (n):

$n = NPQ$ divided by $[(N-1)D + PQ]$
$n = 200$ divided by $[0.5202 + 0.25] = 260$

Interpretation

These results suggest that a random sample of 260 teachers is needed to get an estimate of the percent of all 800 teachers who would give a yes response to the questionnaire item. In this sampling design, the margin of error will *not* exceed 5 percent.

Table B. Margin of error for Problem 1.2.

Step One:	$pq = (0.85) (0.15) = 0.1275$
Step Two:	$U = 0.1275/260 = 0.000490$
Step Three:	$F = (800 - 260)/800 = 0.6750$
Step Four:	$V = (U) (F) = 0.000331$
Step Five:	$S =$ Square Root of $V = 0.0182$
Step Six:	$M = (1.96) (0.0182) = 0.036$ (or 3.6 percent)

Interpretation

The margin of error for this survey is 3.6 percent. These results have the following interpretation: we are 95 percent certain that the true percent of all 800 teachers who would give a yes response to the questionnaire item is between 81.4 percent and 88.6 percent.

Table C. Common standard deviation for Problem 2.1.

Step One:	A = 200 − 1 = 199
Step Two:	B = (199) (121) = 24,079
Step Three:	C = 200 − 1 = 199
Step Four:	D = (199) (81) = 16,119
Step Five:	E = 24,079 + 16,199 = 40,198
Step Six:	F = 199 + 199 = 398
Step Seven:	G = 19,998 divided by 198 = 101
Step Eight:	H = Square Root of 101 = 10.05

Interpretation

   In this example, the common standard deviation is 10.05. This common standard deviation is used with the sample mean difference to get the effect size for evaluating the results of the Algebra I experiment. See Table D.

Table D. Effect size for Problem 2.2.

Formula

ES = SMD divided by CSD
ES = (89 − 79) divided by 10.05 = 1.00

Legend

   ES = the effect size estimate
   SMD = the sample mean differences
   CSD = the common standard deviation

Interpretation

   Given the Algebra I experiment having a 10-point sample mean difference favoring students taught by Method One, and a common standard deviation equal to 10.05 points, the effect size estimate is 1.00. This effect size estimate has the following interpretation:

   On average, students taught by Method One have performance scores that are 1.0 standard deviations higher than the performance scores for students taught by Method Two.

Table E. Responses for Problem 2.3.

Question One: Which method was the more effective strategy for teaching Algebra I?

Response: Given that the Algebra I experiment had an effect size value of 1.00 favoring Method One, the new teaching method was clearly more effective than the traditional teaching method (Method Two).

Question Two: How would you communicate this difference to policymakers and practitioners without reference to technical statistical terms?

Response: An examination of Table 2./ indicates that an effect size value of 1.00 has a 34 percent advantage. With this information in hand, the experimental results can be summarized as follows:

First, indicate that 50 percent of the Algebra I students exposed to Method Two (the school district's traditional teaching method) had achievement scores **equal to or above 79** (which is the average achievement score for this experimental group).

Next, indicate that 84 percent of the Algebra I students exposed to Method One (the new teaching method) had achievement scores **equal to or above 79** (which is the average achievement score the school district was likely to get if the new teaching method was not introduced in this experimental study).

Therefore, it is correct to state the following experimental conclusion: **The Algebra I experiment suggests that an additional 34 percent of all Algebra I students in the school distirct would equal or exceed the typical (historical average) achievement score of 79 if just the new method of teaching (Method One) was used next year.**

JAMES F. MCNAMARA (Ph.D., Penn State, 1970) is a professor at Texas A&M University. He holds graduate faculty appointments in the Departments of Statistics, Educational Psychology, and Educational Administration. Prior to joining the Texas A&M faculty in 1976, he held professorial appointments at Columbia University and the University of Oregon. While at Texas A&M, he has been a Visiting Scholar at the University of Michigan (1979) and an Advanced Study Center Fellow at Ohio State University (1980).

Before pursuing a career in higher education, Dr. McNamara spent three years as a high school mathematics teacher in New Jersey and four years as an administrator in the Research Bureau of the Pennsylvania Department of Public Instruction. Earlier in his career, he worked in several corporations including Trans World Airlines, Philco-Ford, and VERTOL Helicopter. He also completed a three-year tour of duty in the U.S. Army Corps of Engineers.

As an educational policy researcher, Dr. McNamara has published more than eighty research articles and policy reports. For his article on the use of statistical models in educational research, he received the Best Research Manuscript Award from the *Journal of Industrial Teacher Education.* He has also appeared as an expert witness on educational desegregation policies before the U.S. District Court (Houston, TX), and he has delivered several invited research lectures to organizations such as the National Academy of School Executives, the Rand Corporation (Santa Monica, CA), and the Interamerican Congress of Psychology (Caracus, Venezuela).

Dr. McNamara was a Co-Founder and the Executive Director of the Texas A&M School/University Research Collaborative. Founded in 1986, this cooperative research organization brought school district and university research colleagues together to work on instructional and administrative problems of mutual interest. Under his leadership, the Collaborative developed a national reputation for conducting informative policy research studies that assist individual school districts to design and implement more effective student dropout prevention programs. For these contributions to collaborative educational research, he received a 1990 Faculty Research Award from the Instructional Research Laboratory at Texas A&M University.